# BASIC UNITED METHODIST BELIEFS

## AN EVANGELICAL VIEW

Edited by

**James V. Heidinger II**

**BRISTOL BOOKS**

**Basic United Methodist Beliefs**
Copyright © 1986 by A Forum for Scriptural Christianity, Inc.

First Printing, January 1986
Second Printing, June 1986
Third Printing, August 1988
Fourth Printing, April 1990
Fifth Printing, February 1992
Sixth Printing, March 1993
Seventh Printing, June 1994
Eighth Printing, January 1995
Ninth Printing, August 1995
Tenth Printing, April 1996
Eleventh Printing, October 1997
Twelfth Printing, October 1998
Thirteenth Printing, March 2000
Fourteenth Printing, March 2001
Fifteenth Printing, March 2002
Sixteenth Printing, September 2002
Seventeenth Printing, April 2004
Eighteenth Printing, September 2005
Nineteenth Printing, January 2007
Twentieth Printing, July 2007

Unless otherwise indicated, all Scripture quotations are from the *New American Standard Bible*, © 1960, 1962, 1963, 1971, 1973, 1975, 1977 by the Lockman Foundation. Used by permission.

All rights reserved. Except for brief quotations embodied in critical articles and reviews, no part of this book may be used or reproduced in any manner whatsoever without written permission.

Printed in the United States of America.

Library of Congress Catalog Card Number: 86-80014
ISBN: 0-917851-01-3
Suggested Subject Heading: Methodist Doctrine
Recommended Dewey Decimal Classification: 230:7

**BRISTOL BOOKS**
An Imprint of Bristol House, Ltd.
1201 E. 5th St., Suite 2107
Anderson, IN 46012
Phone: 765-644-0856 Fax: 765-622-1045
To order call: 1-800-451-READ (7323)
**www.bristolhouseltd.com**

# Table of Contents

Preface .......................................................... 1

Chapter 1    "Let's Rediscover Wesley for Our
Time"—Dennis F. Kinlaw................. 5

Chapter 2    "Wesley On Scripture"
—Mack B. Stokes............................ 12

Chapter 3    "The Wesleyan Quadrilateral—Not
Equilateral"—Robert G. Tuttle, Jr...... 19

Chapter 4    "How Sin Got In and Why It Won't Go
Away"—Riley B. Case..................... 26

Chapter 5    "Who Is Jesus?"—Paul A. Mickey......... 32

Chapter 6    "Cross Purposes: Wesley's View of the
Atonement"—Steve Harper............... 39

Chapter 7    "Saved by Faith, Saved by Works, or
Why Be Saved at All?"—James V.
Heidinger II.................................... 46

*Basic United Methodist Beliefs: An Evangelical View*

Chapter 8    "Nobody's Perfect, Right?"—William B.
             Coker............................................... 54
Chapter 9    "I Will Build My Church"—Frank
             Bateman Stanger.............................. 63
Chapter 10   "Wesley's Principles For Social
             Action"—Frank Baker...................... 72
Chapter 11   "The Lord's Supper in the Wesleyan
             Tradition"—John R. Tyson................ 80
Chapter 12   "Ready For His Return"—Joel B. Green  90
Chapter 13   "How Revival Comes"—Robert E.
             Coleman........................................ 98
Appendix A   "The Junaluska Affirmation of Scriptural
             Christianity for United Methodists".....107
Appendix B   "The Character of a Methodist"—John
             Wesley.......................................... 115

# Preface

In 1972 the United Methodist General Conference adopted a new doctrinal statement entitled "Our Theological Task." The statement introduced United Methodists to the new affirmation of "theological pluralism," a formal recognition of United Methodism's broad doctrinal diversity. The statement was also an indicator of our theological uncertainty.

Some United Methodists viewed theological pluralism as a great strength, while others felt its liabilities far exceeded any strengths. But without question, the new doctrinal statement did not provide clear guidance for United Methodists as to what their church affirmed theologically.

In the March/April 1983 issue of *Good News* magazine, we began a series of articles on the Wesleyan doctrinal distinctives. Our goal was to help clarify what United Methodists believe. We also wanted to help our readers rediscover John Wesley in a

1

fresh, contemporary way. The magazine series coincided with plans for the approaching bicentennial celebration of Methodism in America, which brought with it a resurgence of interest in Methodist theology.

We asked a variety of well-known United Methodist leaders, writers, and teachers to contribute to the series. Though coming from different backgrounds, the participants all are evangelical in their faith and theological commitment. This book, with the exception of one chapter, is a compilation of the magazine series.

This volume gives a fresh, readable introduction to basic United Methodist beliefs. It is faithful to both the Scripture and our Methodist tradition. The multiplicity of contributors gives the work a variety of writing styles and provides the reader with at least a few names that will be familiar.

The book has 13 chapters, making it ideal for a quarter's study in the church school. The questions for discussion at the end of each chapter will be helpful for the teacher or group leader, as well as the individual reader. Chapter lengths are manageable enough to make the book right for an evening study group or a supplemental resource for adult confirmation classes.

We have included as an appendix the full text of "The Junaluska Affirmation," a statement of Scriptural Christianity adopted by Good News in 1975. The Junaluska Affirmation was Good News' response to the mandate given the United Methodist Church in the new doctrinal statement adopted by the 1972 General Conference, which urged all members "to accept the challenge of responsible theological reflection."

So in April, 1974, the Good News Board of Directors appointed a "Theology and Doctrine Task Force" to prepare an affirmative statement of Scriptural Christianity. On July 20, 1975, "An Affirmation of Scriptural Christianity for United Methodists" was adopted by the Good News Board of Directors meeting at Lake Junaluska, North Carolina. We

hope the Junaluska Affirmation will assist you in your own theological reflection.

In 1980, *Essentials of Wesleyan Theology* was published, written by Paul A. Mickey, associate professor of pastoral theology at the Duke University Divinity School. Mickey's book is an in-depth commentary on The Junaluska Affirmation and provides a systematic approach to theology from the Wesleyan/Arminian perspective.

In a second appendix, we have included as an additional resource the Good News paraphrase of "The Character of a Methodist," John Wesley's profound and popular definition of the Methodist character.

Many United Methodists were encouraged that the 1984 General Conference authorized a task force to prepare a new doctrinal statement for the church. Good News welcomes this new theological emphasis because we believe that the evangelical renewal of our church will not happen apart from a corresponding renewal of her historic and Scriptural theology.

We pray that this book will help spark renewed interest in doctrinal study all across United Methodism. Such a new interest, if widespread enough, could help bring lasting spiritual and theological renewal to the United Methodist Church.

James V. Heidinger II, Editor
*Good News* magazine
308 East Main Street
Wilmore, Kentucky 40390

# 1

# Let's Rediscover Wesley for Our Time

by
Dennis F. Kinlaw

**S**ome years ago I was talking with a neighboring United Methodist pastor about the then-current theological scene. I noted there seemed to be a renewed interest within Methodism in the theology of John Wesley. I registered my pleasure. I was somewhat surprised when my friend assured me that he could envision few prospects more dismal to him than a return by the church to the theology of its founder.

That conversation reflects one of the perpetual tensions within the church. How does one generation of Christians relate to the beliefs of a previous one? Or better, how does the present UM Church relate to its origins? Do we maintain the historic dogmas [doctrines]? Or, does God have a new Word for every age that makes the past Word irrelevant? Is the study of Wesley a dated exercise, or does such study contain potential for renewal?

Continuity and change are equally evident in Biblical faith. Basic truths and transitions producing newer understandings are integral to the development of our historic Christian faith. In light of this truth the need to rediscover Wesley becomes apparent.

Methodism's founder had a full understanding of the central doctrines of historic Christian orthodoxy. Yet he was open to newer understandings of Christian thought and helped to enlarge that understanding to an amazingly broad spectrum of living. Undoubtedly, this is why serious study of Wesley is in resurgence today. The Wesleyan distinctives are worthy of rediscovery.

My students recently came to grips with the growth of doctrine in the first five centuries of the Church. Many found it exciting, surprising, and satisfying. Most had never seen how the Church dealt with the mysteries of the Christian faith and how deeper understanding of the truths of Scripture came only with *time* and *work*.

The early Church had the Bible. Having it, though, did not mean fully understanding God's rich revelation.

Take for an example the doctrine of the nature of Christ and His relationship to the Father. It is easy for us to think and to speak of the deity of Christ. It is another matter to understand the massive battles of mind and heart that had to be waged before that which seems obvious to us could even be thought.

If someone could have asked the Apostle Paul if he believed in the Holy Trinity, what do you think would have been his response? It might well have been a perplexed, "I beg your pardon?" The word "trinity" was not to occur on Christian lips for a century after Paul's martyrdom. His inspired writings were basic to the formulation of that essential Christian doctrine. His writings, though, were basic and authoritative building material, not final definition. Paul was writing letters to early, growing churches; he was not formulating creeds.

6

## THE PROBLEM OF JESUS

Think of the shock to a good Jew who heard his first Christian witness and found there were people who revered Moses and the Hebrew prophets, who worshipped Yahweh, but who also believed God had a son, a real son. That sounded like polytheistic paganism to him. The cardinal doctrine in every synagogue was that Yahweh was One and One alone.

How did the Church resolve the problem of Jesus? He obviously was a man. His crucifixion and burial proved that. Yet, to the early Christian it seemed appropriate to worship Him. In fact, it seemed to be the only adequate response. But what problems!

For the best evidence of the progress of dogma in history, compare the great passages about God in Isaiah with portions of the book of Revelation. Consider John's vision of Heaven. He sees a door opened. Before him is the very throne of God. Cherubim and elders cast their crowns before God and adore Him. Heaven rings with their Trishagion ("Holy, Holy, Holy").

John is spellbound. Then he gets a second look. Standing in the midst of the throne is an equal recipient of adoration, the Lamb slain from the foundation of the world.

It was no irreverent believer who said of this sight, "Mary's baby has come a long way." That is not irreverent because all of our understanding of Christian love, grace, and redemption is tied up with this. The Church insists that in Mary's child, later to become the Paschal sacrifice, it can see both "God *with* us and God *for* us."

But some will say, "That is within Scripture. The Canon is closed now and our doctrine is complete." Let's not forget, though, the development of those early centuries as the Church hammered out its understanding of the nature of that relationship pictured in apocalyptic imagery by John—Jesus on the throne.

That theological discussion and development saved the Church from the sterility of gnosticism on the one hand, in which God never identified Himself with our sin and lostness; and unitarianism on the other, in which Jesus is simply an example for men who could be good if they would.

Edwin Lewis understood this. His word to a group of young preachers was this: "Whether you have a Gospel hangs upon whether you believe that Jesus was the son of Mary who became the Son of God or whether you believe that Jesus was the Son of God who became the son of Mary." To the world this may only suggest a subtle distinction. But to the Church it is the difference between man on his own and man with a Savior.

Protestants believe that further definition in our understanding of Biblical truth has developed since those first five centuries. They dare to think that in Luther and Calvin a cardinal doctrine, the doctrine of justification by faith, reached a clarity of definition not achieved before in any broad sense by the Christian Church.

Does Luther replace the Scripture, or does Luther lead to the rejection of older truth? Obviously not. Luther simply helped us understand more of what was already stated in Scripture and implicit within the classical creeds. Truth always brings freedom. More truth brings more freedom.

### THE WESLEYAN REVIVAL

A similar step in the progress of dogma occurred in the Wesleyan revival. The question now was not saving grace. Rather, it was grace for living, grace for fullness of life. It was not whether we could be forgiven but whether we could have the mind of Christ—whether we could move from fear and duty into the freedom of love. The question was not new, only the context.

Heir to the wisdom of the centuries and grateful recipient of the insights of the reformers, Wesley dutifully pushed the frontiers of Christian questioning and understanding. He saw that all of Christian life is by grace and grace alone. He saw that there is not only grace for the sinner but a fullness of grace even for the believer. The result of this was dramatic.

Nowhere is this better illustrated than in the story of one of Wesley's lay preachers. The preacher had met opposition. Mobbed and stoned, he was finally dragged from the village and rolled in the ditch which served as the community's sewer system. His final comment tells the story: "And I felt nothing but love." Little wonder that the transformation reached beyond individuals to a society.

### WESLEY AND THE ESSENTIALS

Wesley's procedure is instructive for us. He added nothing to Scripture. His concern was to see and make his own what was specifically there. He had no desire to repudiate the dogmas of the past. That would have been folly. Collin Williams is on target when he says Wesley believed there were essential doctrines which are expressive of the Christian's faith.

What were these *essential doctrines*? Original sin, the deity of Christ, the atonement, justification by faith alone, the work of the Holy Spirit, and the Trinity. In other words, Wesley was classically orthodox.

Could he think new thoughts? Yes! But they must be consistent with the old truths.

Thus his interest in the Scripture. He called himself "a man of one Book." One Book was normative. Others were helpful.

### A MODEL FOR TODAY

Is there a model here for us? I think there is. It may well be that the current stagnant state of the church is not due to the fact that the old truths are no longer relevant. In my own travels I have observed that the old truths are unknown. Our sin is not only unbelief. It is also laziness and ignorance.

A rediscovery of the old truths might help us approach again the frontiers of truth. A happy thought, and a sobering one follows: reclaiming the old truths might bring us to a position where we could see some things new.

Why live behind our fathers when it is possible to live ahead? That is God's will. However, we shall find that will happen only when we have been faithful to God's Word, faithful to the truth in our past, and faithful to His call to press forward.

---

**Dennis F. Kinlaw** is chancellor of Asbury College in Wilmore, Kentucky. He also serves on the boards of OMS International and Christianity Today, Inc. He is president of the Francis Asbury Society and the author of *Preaching in the Spirit*.

Prior to his years as a college administrator, Dr. Kinlaw taught the history, theology, and languages of the Old Testament at Asbury Theological Seminary. His Ph.D. is from Brandeis University.

## STUDY GUIDE

1. What might be some of the benefits of a return by the United Methodist Church to the theology of its founder, John Wesley? What might be some of the liabilities?
2. What role should the Bible have in guiding our understanding and application of spiritual truth? What role should the Church have in this process? What examples from the early Church does the author give to illustrate the

respective roles of Scripture and the Church in formulating Christian doctrine?

3. Edwin Lewis said, "Whether you have a Gospel hangs upon whether you believe that Jesus was the son of Mary who became the Son of God or whether you believe that Jesus was the Son of God who became the son of Mary." Do you agree or disagree with this statement? Why?

4. Should the Church today accept new beliefs about God and faith? In what way, if at all, should these new beliefs be related to the "old truths" already accepted by the Church?

5. For what "noble" practice did the Apostle Paul commend the Bereans in regard to the way they judged the "new truths" that came their way? See Acts 17:10-11.

6. According to the author, what was the central Christian truth uncovered by Luther? By Wesley?

7. Wesley believed that six areas of Christian belief are "essential doctrines." What are these six doctrines?

8. Jot down a brief definition for each of the six "essential doctrines." Keep your list with you as you read the rest of this book, and compare your definitions with the way the authors explain each of these doctrines.

9. Look again at the list of "essential doctrines." How might your own perspective and lifestyle change if you made these doctrines an integral part of your philosophy of life? How might your church be affected if these doctrines were emphasized more?

10. Think about the author's closing words: "Why live behind our fathers when it is possible to live ahead? That is God's will. However, we shall find that will happen only when we have been faithful to God's Word, faithful to the truth in our past, and faithful to His call to press forward." Do you agree or disagree? Why or why not?

# 2

# Wesley on Scripture

by

Mack B. Stokes

$\mathbf{F}$or Methodism's founder, the basis for Christian belief and practice was—first, last, and always—the Holy Bible. John Wesley was steeped in Scripture from childhood. He studied the Bible in depth as a student at Oxford. His preaching was based on the Bible. And his guidance to the people called Methodists was derived from the Bible.

Wesley urged his preachers to read not only the Bible but also other books. Yet at the same time, he said the final authority for belief and practice is the Bible.

As Wesley put it: "All faith is founded upon divine authority, so there is now no divine authority but the Scriptures. . ." (John Wesley, *Works*, Vol. X, p. 91). He wrote in his journal: "My ground is the Bible. . . I follow it in all things great and small" (June 5, 1766).

Back of Wesley's commitment to Scripture was his conviction that it shows the way of salvation. "I want to know one thing," said Wesley,"—the way to heaven; how to land safe on that happy shore. God Himself has condescended to teach the way; for this very end He came from heaven. He has written it down in a book. O give me that book! At any price, give me the book of God!" (John Wesley, *Sermons*, Vol. 1, pp. 31-32).

Wesley was determined that his followers should live by the Bible. This was so important to him that he included his views on the authority of Scripture in "The General Rules of Our Society." These principles guided the beliefs of early Methodists. Here Wesley said the Bible is "the only rule, and the sufficient rule, both for our faith and practice."

Wesley flatly stated that the Bible stands above church tradition. Yet he believed that the great traditions of the church are important for interpreting the Bible.

He stated also that the Bible stands above Christian experience. Wesley believed Christian experience backs up the truth of Scripture. He also believed that Scripture should be interpreted in the light of Christian experience—but that Christian experience does not carry equal weight to Scripture. The Bible, not Christian experience, is the final basis for Christian doctrine.

Wesley was well aware that the Bible has to be interpreted. In fact, he knew that no one can read Scripture without bringing to it something of his own interpretation. That's why Wesley taught that tradition, Christian experience, and reason are all helpful in interpreting the Bible.

He realized there would be differences in interpretation among even the most sincere and informed Christians. But most differences among Christians, Wesley believed, usually concern matters that are not essential to salvation and practical Christian living.

Wesley's own interpretation of Scripture dealt primarily with three basic areas of Biblical truth: (1) the Bible's teaching about salvation, (2) its teachings about responsible Christian living and evangelistic outreach, and (3) God's promises and blessings.

### A CRUCIAL TEACHING

Wesley regarded the Biblical teachings on justification and the New Birth as the two most important Christian doctrines (*Sermons*, Vol. II, pp. 226-227). Justification, he said, is God's mighty action through Jesus Christ crucified, whereby our sins are blotted out and the slate is wiped clean. This is God's act *for* us. The New Birth is God's gracious act *in* us whereby we are recreated, born anew, and set on our course toward heaven and toward right living on earth. The New Birth is the beginning of sanctification.

Many people today either ignore Wesley's emphasis on the New Birth or they water it down. But for Wesley, this Biblical teaching was crucial.

The New Birth, he said,

> is the great change which God works in the soul when He brings it into life; when He raises it from the death of sin to the life of righteousness. It is a change wrought in the whole soul by the Almighty Spirit of God when it is created anew in Christ Jesus; when it is renewed after the image of God in righteousness and true holiness; when the love of the world is changed into the love of God; pride into humility; passion into meekness; hatred, envy, malice, into a sincere, tender, disinterested love for all mankind (*Sermons*, Vol. II, p. 234).

It's important to remember that, according to Wesley, both justification and the New Birth are realities only by grace through faith. And he understood the whole process of salvation to involve the direct operation of the Holy Spirit.

Wesley taught that God's great work of salvation is often done suddenly, but it is also a process of spiritual growth. That's why Wesley believed that every Christian must be regular in reading Scripture, in prayer, in public worship, and in service.

When Wesley spoke of being saved by faith alone, he didn't confine this merely to one event or experience. In his essay on

"The Character of a Methodist," he said that salvation means holiness of heart and life. And this, said Wesley, springs from true faith alone.

### RESPONSIBLE CHRISTIAN LIVING AND EVANGELISTIC OUTREACH

This brings us to the second emphasis that John Wesley made in his use of Scripture. It has to do with the connection between the New Birth and its outward expression. Wesley insisted that "inward holiness" requires "outward holiness." To our understanding of this area of Biblical truth, Wesley made a distinctive contribution.

Many people have stressed the inner life. And many others have called attention to the ethical and evangelistic demands of the Gospel. But Wesley brought these together with a fresh, new emphasis.

His teaching on the power of the Holy Spirit within us takes us back to the apostles. His teaching on the Christian action which flows from that supernatural source takes us back to a correct interpretation of law and grace.

God's *law*, taught Wesley, not only makes us aware of our sin; it is to be obeyed. As for *grace*, Wesley pointed to the vast resources that enable us to obey God by manifesting His love in our daily lives.

Today, many recognize the importance of the inner spiritual life. But they don't focus enough on the life-changing presence of the Holy Spirit. Others stress the social gospel and the duties of the Christian for world outreach. But they fail to lift up the power of the Holy Spirit who alone can provide the dynamic for effective social action and evangelism. Wesley kept these elements in unique balance.

### GOD'S PROMISES AND BLESSINGS

A third emphasis in Wesley's interpretation of Scripture concerns the promises and blessings God gives His children when they open their lives to Him in faith and obedience. One of the most important of these is *assurance*, or the witness of the Spirit.

Wesley's idea on this matter, based on Romans 8:15-16 and Galatians 4:6-7, is simply that the Holy Spirit bears witness with our spirits that we are God's children. And every Christian, said Wesley, is entitled to experience this blessed assurance that he or she is a child of God. Wesley regarded the witness of the Spirit as "one grand part of the testimony which God has given [Methodists] to bear to all mankind."

Wesley also emphasized the many other blessings which God has for His children: victory over sin, joy, the peace of God.

For Wesley, one of the greatest blessings possible is a soul filled with the love of Jesus Christ. This blessing is so great because it enables us to overcome hostility, resentment, and an unforgiving spirit. The greatest of all blessings, Wesley believed, is to *know* we have passed from death into life, that we are indeed the children of God.

In all that Wesley taught, he pointed to the Bible as the basis for his beliefs. He never got away from the authority of Scripture. Late in life he reemphasized this conviction when he said about the people called Methodists: "What is their fundamental doctrine? That the Bible is the whole and sole rule of Christian faith and practice" (*Works*, Vol. XIII, p. 258).

---

**Mack B. Stokes**, a retired United Methodist bishop, pastored churches in North Carolina and Georgia, held teaching and administrative posts at Candler School of Theology, and served on several national boards and agencies of the UMC. He was elected bishop in 1972 and assigned to United Methodism's Jackson (Mississippi) Area.

Bishop Stokes has authored many books and articles including *The Bible in the Wesleyan Heritage, Questions*

*Asked by United Methodists,* and *The Holy Spirit in the Wesleyan Heritage.* He received the Ph.D. from Boston University.

## STUDY GUIDE

1. Wesley said, "All faith is founded upon divine authority, so there is now no divine authority but the Scriptures. . . ." What competitors today are challenging the divine authority of the Scriptures?
2. In "The General Rules of Our Society" Wesley said the Bible was "the only rule, and the sufficient rule, both for our faith and practice." Is the Bible that for you today? What are some practical implications of this position?
3. Wesley knew we all bring something of our own backgrounds to our interpretation of Scripture. Discuss the Wesleyan guidelines of tradition, Christian experience, and reason and their role in the interpretation of Scripture.
4. Do you agree with Wesley that most differences in interpretation among Christians usually concern matters not essential to salvation and practical Christian living? Discuss.
5. What does it mean to say, "The Bible, not Christian experience, is the final basis for Christian doctrine?" What are some possible dangers, if any, of making experience finally authoritative?
6. In Wesley's interpretation of the Scripture, he regarded the teachings on justification and the New Birth as the two most important Christian doctrines. Do you agree? Why or why not?
7. Do you believe, as the author says, that Wesley's emphasis on the New Birth is often either ignored or watered down today? If it is, why is it?

8. Another key in Wesley's use of Scripture was the connection he made between the New Birth and outward holiness. Why is it hard for Christians today to keep a balance between these two aspects of the Christian life?

9. A third key in Wesley's interpretation of Scripture was his focus on the promises and blessings God gives His children when they open their lives to Him. One great promise was "assurance" or "the witness of the Spirit." Is it presumptuous to claim we can know we are God's child? Discuss.

10. Look at Romans 8:15-16 and Galatians 4:6-7 regarding the doctrine of assurance. Wesley believed this doctrine was the "one grand part of the testimony which God has given Methodists to bear to all mankind." Has assurance remained a major doctrine in United Methodist teaching today? Discuss.

# 3

# The Wesleyan Quadrilateral—Not Equilateral

## *Putting Scripture, Tradition, Reason, and Experience into Focus*

by
Robert G. Tuttle, Jr.

United Methodists for many years have appealed to Scripture, reason, tradition, and experience. We have called this the Wesley quadrilateral, the source of "our present existing and established standards of doctrine."[1] In 1972 the Wesley quadrilateral first appeared, along with considerable definition, in the doctrinal statement in our *Book of Discipline*. United Methodists refer to it regularly to support a broad swath of Christian teaching.

Unfortunately, we have too frequently understood quadrilateral to mean equilateral, as though there is no principal source on which faith depends. The results have been conflict and inconsistency.

At some points, however, our people deserve a *United* Methodist response to our troubled times to provide direction for the church. We have the right to expect enough compatibility in the understanding of our doctrinal essentials that we do not raise more questions than we answer. If we are ever to be United Methodist, we must realize that quadrilateral does not mean equilateral.

Wesley appealed to Scripture, reason, tradition, and experience when attempting to document and support his own position.[2] But his quadrilateral had a dominant side—Scripture. He fully intended that Scripture take precedent. He wrote in the preface to his standard sermons: "God himself has condescended to teach the way: For this very end he came from heaven. He hath written it down in a book." He then exclaims, "O, give me that book! At any price, give me the book of God! I have it: Here is knowledge enough for me. Let me be *homo unius libri*" (a man of one book).[3]

## THE PRIMACY OF SCRIPTURE

If Wesley was truly a man of one Book (which some have difficulty believing since he used so many different sources), the place to begin is with his view of Scripture.

Wesley insisted that Scripture is the principal authority—the only measure whereby all other truth is tested. In his reply to a Roman catechism he writes: "The Scripture, therefore, is a rule sufficient in itself, and was by men divinely inspired at once delivered to the world; and so neither needs, nor is capable of, any further addition" (*Works,* Vol. X, p. 90).

In 1755 he writes to a friend, Samuel Furly, a general rule for interpreting Scripture: "The literal sense of every text is to be taken, if it be not contrary to some other texts; but in that case, the obscured text is to be interpreted by those which speak more plainly" (*Letters,* Telford ed., Vol. III, p. 129). Here we see not only a reverence for the Word of God, but a healthy guideline for interpretation as well.

The point should be well taken. Any measure for truth must begin with Scripture. Without this focus it is every man for himself; there is no unity of faith. We are "tossed here and there by waves, and carried about by every wind of doctrine"

(Ephesians 4:14). We can reach only so high. If we are to know the truth, then God must stoop to reveal it to us. This brings us to the rest of the quadrilateral. Although Scripture takes precedence, Wesley also clearly appeals to reason, tradition, and experience in support of Scripture.

### REASON, TRADITION, EXPERIENCE

Though Scripture is sufficient unto itself and is the foundation of true religion, Wesley writes: "Now, of what excellent use is reason, if we would either understand ourselves, or explain to others, those living oracles!" (*Works*, Vol. VI, p. 354). He states quite clearly that without reason we cannot understand the essential truths of Scripture. Reason, in this instance however, is not mere human intelligence. It must be assisted by the Holy Spirit if we are to understand the mysteries of God.

Wesley's appreciation for reason not only preceded but extended far beyond Aldersgate. In 1741 he writes of Luther: "How does he decry reason, right or wrong, as an irreconcilable enemy to the Gospel of Christ! Whereas, what is reason (the faculty so called) but the power of apprehending, judging, and discoursing? Which power is no more to be condemned in the gross than seeing, hearing, or feeling" (*Works,* Vol. 1, p. 315).

Yet, in spite of Wesley's profound respect for reason, he was clear as to what reason could and could not do. He knew, for example, that if people were left to themselves they would not reason their way to Heaven, but to hell. Ultimately, reason in and of itself falls short; it is a rope of sand.

In his sermon, "The Case of Reason Impartially Considered," Wesley sought to demonstrate the complete inability of reason to produce faith. He stated: "Although it is always consistent with reason, yet reason cannot produce faith, in the scriptural sense of the word. Faith, according to Scripture, is 'an evidence,' or conviction, 'of things not seen.' It is a divine evidence bringing a full conviction of an invisible, eternal world" (*Works*, Vol. VI, p. 355). Reason, even in its highest

21

state of improvement, could never produce a firm conviction in anyone's mind.

Although Wesley persisted in his own appreciation for reason throughout his life, he insisted that God be on the throne of grace as the one who takes the initiative in the drama of rescue. Reason can do much with regard to both the foundation and the superstructure of religion. Ultimately, however, reason can produce neither faith, hope, nor love. These are gifts of God.

As for tradition, Wesley writes that it is generally supposed that traditional evidence is weakened by length of time. Of necessity it passes through many hands in a continued succession of ages. Although other evidence is perhaps stronger, he insists: "I do not undervalue traditional evidence. Let it have its place and its due honour. It is highly serviceable in its kind, and in its degree" (*Works,* Vol. X, p. 75).

Wesley objected to the Catholic view that tradition is absolute truth. However, he does admit that men of strong and clear understanding should be aware of the full force of tradition. Like reason, tradition must not be given equal weight with Scripture. Wesley does emphasize the link tradition supplies through 1700 years of history with Jesus and the Apostles. It is an unbroken chain drawing us into fellowship with those who have finished the race, fought the fight, and who now reign with God in His glory and might.

Experience (apart from Scripture) is the strongest proof of Christianity. Wesley quotes, "'What the Scripture promises, I enjoy. Come and see what Christianity has done here. . .'" (*Works,* Vol. X, p. 79). He insisted that we cannot have reasonable assurance of something unless we have experienced it personally. John Wesley was assured of both justification and sanctification because he had experienced them in his own life. "What Christianity (considered as a doctrine) promised, is accomplished in my soul. And Christianity, considered as an inward principle, is the completion of all these promises" (*Works,* Vol. X, p. 75).

Although traditional proof is complex, experience is simple: "One thing I do know, that whereas I was blind, now I see" (John 9:25). Tradition establishes the evidence a long way off; experience makes it present to all persons. As for the proof of Christian doctrine, Wesley states that Christianity is an experience of "holiness and happiness, the image of God impressed on a created spirit; a fountain of peace and love springing up into everlasting life" (*Works*, Vol. X, p. 75).

### The Proper Perspective

We either begin with Scripture which is then served by reason, tradition, and experience; or we begin with reason, tradition, and experience as served by Scripture. Can we reach God out of our own humanity or, ultimately, must He stoop to reveal Himself to us? Wesley believed that God must stoop to reveal Himself to us.

If our United Methodist interpretation of the Wesley quadrilateral is to be true to Wesley then we, too, must begin with Scripture. Again, quadrilateral does not imply equal emphasis even in a pluralistic church. A clear understanding of just how we arrive at doctrine is most important.

Of course, we will not agree on all things. But concerning matters which strike at the root of Christianity we must have some agreement lest we scatter our United Methodist constituents abroad without the common cord to keep them in fellowship one with another. Sometimes there is not a great distance between grinding the ax and burying the hatchet. I hope that this is interpreted as the latter. Surely we owe United Methodists (if not Wesley himself) that much and more.

[1]*The Book of Discipline*, 1980. Page 78.
[2]John Wesley, *Works*. 3rd edition. Volume X, pages 75-79.
[3]*Works*, Vol. V, p. 3.

**Robert G. Tuttle, Jr**. is the E. Stanley Jones professor of evangelism at Garrett-Evangelical Theological Seminary. A member of the Rocky Mountain Annual Conference, he has pastored churches in Illinois, North Carolina, and Colorado. Among his published works are the books, *The Partakers; John Wesley: His Life and Theology; On Giant Shoulders;* and "The Charismatic Renewal in Historical Perspective" a background paper included in *Guidelines for the Charismatic Renewal,* which was approved by the 1976 General Conference of the United Methodist Church.

Before joining the Garrett faculty, Dr. Tuttle taught at the Oral Roberts University School of Theology and before that at Fuller Theological Seminary. He is a graduate of Duke University, Garrett-Evangelical Theological Seminary, Wheaton Graduate School and received the Ph.D. from the University of Bristol.

## STUDY GUIDE

1. What four elements make up the Wesleyan Quadrilateral?
2. Did Wesley consider each element of the quadrilateral equal in importance? If not, which one was most important?
3. Why did Wesley call himself a "man of one book"? Did this mean the Bible was the only book he read?
4. If Scripture is God's Word, why did Wesley also recommend the use of reason, tradition, and experience?
5. Can reason alone bring someone to faith in Christ? Why or why not?
6. Identify at least one hypothetical example of a religious tradition coming into conflict with Scripture. What should be the church's and its members' response in such cases?
7. In what way does tradition "prove" Christianity? Does everyone need to "experience God"?

8. If United Methodists consider the four elements of the quadrilateral as equal, how might such a view hinder understanding of God's will?
9. Brainstorm some ways the four elements of the Wesleyan Quadrilateral might be applied to a current issue facing the denomination.
10. Did Wesley want his followers to use reason, tradition, and experience in order to *add* to Scripture or *interpret* Scripture?

# 4

# How Sin Got In

## *And Why It Won't Go Away*

by

Riley B. Case

I gave copies of "The Articles of Religion" of the United Methodist Church to my adult membership class and asked them to select those articles (or teachings) that are most important and vital to the Christian faith. For the most part the class did well, mentioning articles that explained the Trinity, the Deity of Christ, the Resurrection of Christ, and the Holy Spirit. But not one in the class of eight selected the article of Original Sin.

> Original sin . . . is the corruption of the nature of every man, that naturally is engendered of the offspring of Adam, whereby man is very far gone from original righteousness, and of his own nature inclined to evil, and that continually (Article VII, "The Articles of Religion," p. 57, *Discipline*).

Like many United Methodists, my class members had

overlooked one of the most important doctrines, not only of the United Methodist Church, but of the Church universal. John Wesley would have been appalled at this oversight. For Wesley, the doctrine of original sin was one of the essentials of the Christian faith. He even went so far as to suggest that those who denied this doctrine could not be called Christians:

> All who deny this, call it 'original sin' or by any other title, are but heathen still, in the fundamental point which differences heathenism from Christianity. . . Is man by nature filled with all manner of evil? Is he void of all good? Is he wholly fallen? Is his soul totally corrupted? Or to come back to the [Biblical] text, is 'every imagination of the thoughts of his heart only evil continually'? Allow this, and you are so far a Christian. Deny it, and you are but a heathen still (from the sermon "Original Sin," by John Wesley).

How could Wesley argue that those who do not believe in the doctrine of original sin are not Christians at all?

To answer this, it is important to understand that the doctrine of original sin is not primarily a teaching about sin. For example, what is the best definition of sin? Nor is original sin a doctrine about the first sin: Was there really a man named Adam?

Rather, the doctrine is basically a teaching about *human nature*. That is why, in discussions of Christian belief, the doctrine of original sin is often treated under the heading "Humanity" or the "Doctrine of Man."

A doctrine of man must deal with some very basic questions: Who am I? Where did I come from? Where am I going?

EVOLUTION AND SCIENCE

Much of the modern world answers these questions with a reference to evolution and science: man is the most highly evolved and most complex of all the creatures in the animal world. According to this view, I best understand myself as a combination of heredity, environment, and personal choice. So if I have problems in my life, it's because I inherited a tendency for obesity from my mother, or my father spanked me too hard when I was a child.

Whatever caused me to be the way I am, the world sees the answer to my problem in such approaches as better education, improved technology, or a different political party in power. Absent in this view is any talk about *sin*, or real guilt, or divine judgment.

Wesley called this point of view heathenism. We might call it secular humanism. Some even argue that this view of humanity functions as a *religion*. After all, they point out, secular humanism has a doctrine of origins (evolution and natural selection), and a doctrine of sin (environmental and hereditary deficiency), and a doctrine of salvation (more and better education and technology).

Christians have a different explanation for the human condition. The explanation is linked with the Biblical account of Creation and the Fall found in Genesis 1-3. The Bible teaches that we humans were created good, in the image of God, in order to enjoy fellowship with God. But through the sin of our first parents, that fellowship has been broken by a conscious act of rebellion. As a result, our first parents "fell" from favor with God, and their sin has affected all their children.

We learn from this Bible teaching that human beings are understood and defined by their relationship to God. God has made us, has placed us in this world for a purpose, and holds our destiny in His hands. But we fall short of fulfilling that purpose.

### GOOD AND EVIL

We are a strange mixture of good and evil. On the one hand we are the highest of God's creation, made in His image, capable of love and fellowship, and bestowed with many natural gifts.

On the other hand we do not naturally glorify Him as God. The image of God within us is blurred. Our basic disposition is to use our gifts and abilities, not for God and for others, but for self. As someone has said, "When we're doing what comes naturally, we're not loving our neighbor as ourselves."

Furthermore, we cannot make ourselves righteous by more education, or by creating a better environment, or by an act of our wills. Those who say they don't need Christ or the Church in order to live good, moral lives simply fail to deal with the reality of fallen man. In spite of all our knowledge and sophistication, our inhumanity to each other—as individuals and as nations—is just as cruel today as it was during the time of Christ. Even our best efforts are characterized by selfish motives.

As the *Junaluska Affirmation* (which serves as a doctrinal statement for Good News) says:

> Since the Fall of Adam the corruption of sin has pervaded every person and extended into social relationships, societal systems, and all creation. This corruption is so pervasive that we are not capable of positive response to God's offer of redemption, except by the prevenient, or preparing, grace of God ("Humanity," *The Junaluska Affirmation*).

To some people the doctrine of original sin sounds overly pessimistic. They argue that it makes men and women sound too terrible, as if God doesn't like people. They argue that it leaves religious people with a deep sense of guilt and unworthiness that contributes to emotional and mental health problems.

The Christian counters by saying that original sin is real and guilt is real. But the good news of the Gospel is that, in spite of my sin, God loves me and has sent Jesus Christ to save me from my sin. Even when I am not in right relationship with God, I am of inestimable worth. God cares so much for me that His Son Jesus Christ was willing to lay down His life for me. In Christ, sin is cancelled and I am made a new creature.

Instead of being pessimists, early Methodists were unconquerable optimists. Preaching on sin only set the stage so that the drama of God's grace might be revealed in all its glory.

When persons recognize that the real problem in their lives is sin, they can be led to the real solution, which is Jesus Christ. No matter how pervasive or how *original* sin is, it can be overcome and persons can become new creations in Christ. And if individuals can be changed, there is no reason why society cannot be changed. That kind of gospel is exciting.

By contrast, the real pessimists are the people who deny original sin. When sin is denied, the grace of God that overcomes sin is also denied. Then there is good reason to be pessimistic, not only about individual lives, but about the world's future.

The classical, evangelical Christian view, which understands the doctrine of original sin, is still the most realistic assessment of humanity and the world condition. Biblical Christianity offers humanity's best hope for a better life, both now and in the future.

---

**Riley B. Case** is senior pastor of St. Luke's United Methodist Church in Kokomo, Indiana. A graduate of Taylor University and Garrett-Evangelical Seminary, he has written for numerous publications including *Christian Advocate, Good News,* and *Circuit Rider.* He is the author of *Understanding Our New United Methodist Hymnal* and the popular confirmation resource for United Methodists, *We Believe*, published by Bristol Books.

Riley has been on his conference's Council on Ministries and Board of Ordained Ministry, and was a delegate to the 1984 and 1988 General Conferences. He also served as a consultant for the Hymnal Revision Committee for the New United Methodist Hymnal.

## STUDY GUIDE

1. To what does the word "original" in the term "original sin" refer?
2. Do you agree with Wesley's statement that a person who denies the doctrine of original sin is still a "heathen"? Why did Wesley believe this?
3. In what sense are persons born sinful?
4. Is it possible for a person never to sin?
5. Would better education solve the problem of humanity's sinfulness? Why or why not?
6. Should the doctrine of original sin make people feel pessimistic about themselves and the future? Why or why not?
7. What is the solution to original sin?
8. In what ways does humanity's in-born sinfulness affect society and culture?
9. What commonly held secularist view of why people do bad things is described by the author?
10. Do you believe that babies are affected by original sin? Are small children responsible for the sins they commit?

# 5

# Who Is Jesus?

by
Paul A. Mickey

The question of who is Jesus is one which United Methodists need to answer. Much of American Methodism has moved away from the historic understanding of God's objective revelation in Jesus Christ. This transition has undercut the classical Christian and Wesleyan understanding of who Jesus is.

We need to declare today that Jesus is more than the perfect teacher, moral example, compassionate preacher, or lovable wonder-worker. He may be all of these, but above all He is the Son of God. Through Jesus alone we have access to God the Father.

Jesus' relation to humanity may be seen as a two-way bridge which spans the gulf between God and the world. There is no other way, name, or means under heaven by which that connection between a holy God and a sinful world can be established (Acts 4:12; John 14:6).

## JESUS: GOD AND MAN

The first span of the bridge touches earth in the virgin birth of Jesus (Matthew 1:18-25; Luke 1:26-38). Belief in His virgin birth is vital. It affirms that God was incarnate in the infant son, Jesus of Nazareth. It affirms that Jesus was a part of the Godhead before His birth as a human being. In the virgin birth of Jesus Christ, God put on human flesh.

Yet earth was not Jesus' original home. Before the beginning of time He was one with the Father and the Holy Spirit (Genesis 1; John 1). These three together make up *the Trinity*.

John Wesley compared the Trinity to the merging flame of three candles. When you look at the flame itself you only see one source of light. But looking more closely, you see three candles, each with its own identity. Another way to think of the Trinity is as a triangle, a figure that would be incomplete unless all three corners and sides were present and connected.

Ultimately we cannot prove the Trinity by logic. We accept it by faith. But it is a faith that leads to understanding. The Bible affirms our knowledge of the Trinity, and the Holy Spirit illuminates it.

The phrase "truly God and truly man" is often used to affirm that Jesus Christ is equally divine and human. Jesus was not merely a wise and caring teacher, a countryside preacher and spiritual handyman who did lots of miracles. Nor was He some kind of spiritual essence floating around in carpenter's clothes. He was not pure spirit. He needed sleep, food, love, and baths.

Jesus is *both* God and man. He is the supreme representative of heaven and earth. Without this affirmation one end or the other of the heaven-and-earth bridge would not be firmly planted.

In the Old Testament God revealed His purposes for humanity through *prophets*, *priests*, and *kings*. The prophets included Isaiah, Jeremiah, Amos, and Hosea. Among the priests were Aaron and Samuel. The kings included David and Jehoshaphat. God used these three distinct avenues to establish righteousness and to bring about repentance and forgiveness.

But all these strands of partial revelation were combined in the person of Jesus, God's only begotten Son. No longer does humanity need a prophet, priest, or king to mediate God's will and intention. In Jesus all avenues flow into the one new bridge—with two-way, non-stop traffic between heaven and earth.

JESUS: THE SAVIOR

Why does humanity need such a bridge?

The gulf between heaven and earth opened in the Garden of Eden. The perfect, complete fellowship that Adam (Hebrew for human being) had with God was broken through sin (Genesis 3). And Adam and Eve were stranded on the sinful, earthside of the gulf.

*Original sin* produced the chasm which exists between God and man. We all live under its curse. We cannot have fellowship with God unless we have a mediator, a bridge over the chasm.

But in spite of God's provision in Jesus Christ, man has never quit trying to build the bridge from his sinful side of the gulf. Such efforts, "good works" we call them, will never be successful. In fact, they make matters worse, because they hinder us from trusting in God's grace extended through Jesus Christ. The bridge of salvation had to be built from the heaven side of the sin chasm, not the good-works side.

We fail to see God's provision in Christ because of the blinding effects of Adam's fall. So, through what John Wesley called *prevenient* (or preparing) *grace*, God sends the third member of the Trinity to make our hearts and lives receptive to Jesus Christ.

The Holy Spirit has to awaken us to an awareness that we are sinners in need of forgiveness. To accomplish this, the Holy Spirit crosses the chasm and establishes a small beachhead in our lives. He clears the underbrush, helping us see through our sin, pride, vanity, desperation, and fear; so we can recognize and respond to God's grace in Jesus.

Our sin prevents us from seeing Jesus Christ as the bridge

between God and man. And we may die in the fog banks of our own sin, while standing next to the wide open bridge of salvation.

Or, through the work of the Holy Spirit, we can be saved by faith in Christ. As the Holy Spirit stirs us to spiritual awareness, we can repent of our sins and by faith take the first steps onto the bridge. But we cannot see the other side; we must walk by faith (Ephesians 2:8; I Corinthians 13:12). All God asks us to do is trust the grace offered us in Jesus Christ, through His atoning death on the cross.

When we step onto the bridge we become a part of Christ and He comes to live in us (Galatians 2:20). But none of this can happen unless we accept the fact that Jesus died in our place, confess that He was crucified for our sins, and trust in Him for our salvation.

All of this is given through the unmerited grace of God. The Holy Spirit prepares us, the death of Christ redeems us, and the open invitation to begin a new life in Jesus is offered to us.

### JESUS: EVER WITH US

God's work in us is not complete at the time of our initial salvation. When Jesus closed His ministry on earth He promised to send His followers a Comforter or Counselor, the Holy Spirit, to be with them (John 15-16; Acts 1-2). Through the power of the Holy Spirit we are able to make progress in our new life in Christ.

Further, in the sacraments of Holy Communion and Baptism, Jesus continues to be present with us through the Holy Spirit. The sacraments call the believer and the local congregation to continue walking on the bridge of faith. The sacraments are also means by which we offer thanksgiving to God for His grace.

### JESUS: GOOD SHEPHERD

The lost sheep of the world have their view of the heaven-and-earth bridge blocked. Their view is obscured by their personal sins as well as the sins of society in general. Poor health, wrong living, oppression, and alienation are all rooted in the sins of this world. They are manifestations of the curse of original sin.

The believer has an obligation to reach out in the name of Jesus, becoming a co-worker with Him, the Good Shepherd of the lost. When we receive Christ it is not so we can float away in some spiritual mist. Rather, we must be inviting others to join in the fellowship of redeemed sinners saved by grace (II Corinthians 5:18-20).

### JESUS: COMING AGAIN

Jesus, who was from the beginning with God the Father, became incarnate as Mary's virgin-born Child. He died for our sins and was raised from the dead. He ascended into heaven. That same Jesus is coming again.

His second coming, long promised by the Scriptures, is the hope of all who believe in Him. It will signal the final victory of the Triune God over the forces of evil, Satan, and his followers.

The final judgment will be a separation of the saved from the damned. God's victory will be complete and all powers and dominions will be subjected to the authority of the Godhead in the name of Jesus Christ (Colossians 1:15-20). The new heaven and the new earth, then fully and completely linked by the two-way bridge, will stand as a glorious witness to God's final triumph in Jesus Christ.

---

**Paul A. Mickey** is associate professor of pastoral theology at the Duke University Divinity School. His published works include the books *Essentials of Wesleyan Theology, Tough Marriage, Marriage and the Middle Years,* and *Breaking Free*

*From Wedlock Deadlock.*

An elder in the North Carolina Annual Conference, Paul relaxes by flying airplanes. (He is a FAA certified instrument flight instructor and pilot.) He is a graduate of Harvard University and Princeton Theological Seminary, where he received the Ph.D.

## STUDY GUIDE

1. "Jesus' relation to humanity," says the author, "may be seen as a two-way bridge which spans the gulf between God and the world." Explain this two-way bridge. How do Acts 4:12 and John 14:6 illustrate this idea?
2. What produced the chasm that exists between God and humanity?
3. What is the significance of Jesus' virgin birth?
4. The Bible teaches that Jesus is both God and man. What is His predominant characteristic, in your opinion? What Bible passages support your perception? Discuss.
5. How do good works function in bridging the chasm between man and God?
6. Of what significance is the Holy Spirit in bridging the chasm between God and man?
7. According to the author, in order to be restored to right relationship with God, what fact must we accept? What must we confess? In whom must we trust?
8. Does initial salvation complete God's work in us? Why or why not?
9. Why are Holy Communion and Baptism important sacraments for the believer?
10. "The believer has an obligation to reach out in the name of Jesus to become a co-worker with Him. . . ." As an individual and as a church body, how can you more

effectively present Christ to others? Brainstorm some ways in which you are and can be the Good Shepherd's co-worker.

# 6

# Cross Purposes

## *Wesley's View of the Atonement*

by

Steve Harper

To the minds of many there is something illogical, even offensive, in the thought that the death of Jesus Christ nearly 2,000 years ago could have any effect upon us today. Part of the problem is the difficulty of seeing a connection with any historical event separated from us by 20 centuries. Further, many people simply do not believe they are sinners. The idea of an atonement on their behalf is repulsive.

People in the 18th century had the same problems. Objections abounded then as now. John Wesley wrote, "Undoubtedly, as long as the world stands, there will be a thousand objections to this Scriptural doctrine. For still the preaching of *Christ crucified* will be foolishness to the wise men of the world" (*Letters*). Yet despite these objections, Wesley's sermons were salted with references to the Cross and Christ's atoning work.

Wesley went so far as to say, "Nothing in the Christian system is of greater consequence than the doctrine of the Atonement. It is properly the distinguishing point between deism and Christianity" (*Letters*). With these words Wesley revealed the importance of the Cross in the Christian faith and the early Methodist movement.

We do well to examine its significance for us today.

The Atonement, we should note, is "the distingushing point" between Christianity and paganism in several key areas.

1. *The Atonement is the distinguishing point concerning the state of humanity.* The Cross is a dramatic reminder that the world is sinful and separated from God. George Croft Cell saw clearly that Wesley's view of the Atonement undercut "a godless humanistic religion. . . . Its master aim is to magnify the grace of God and to bring every man, a sinner in need of a savior, in utter humility to the foot of the cross of Christ" (*The Rediscovery of John Wesley*).

God takes no delight in needless sacrifice. If we believe this, then the Cross must forever be the world's sobering proof that it is headed away from God's purpose for it. If we are not fallen, there is no need for redemption. Self-salvation, too, is out of the question. If we can save ourselves, there is no need of a savior.

## A RADICAL FLAW

No one has commented on this truth more clearly than Dr. Albert Outler in his book, *Theology in the Wesleyan Spirit*. He interprets Wesley's doctrine of sin as "a human flaw that is radical, inescapable, universal—a human malaise that cannot be cured or overcome by any of our self-help efforts as ethical virtues, however 'moral' or aspiring."

Our society may continue to ignore or even redefine sin. It may even erase the word from the language of sophisticated people. But as long as one cross stands atop just one church steeple, it will be a reminder that mankind is hopelessly sinful and in need of a salvation which only God can provide.

2. *The Atonement properly distinguishes the nature of God.* Skeptics who make light of human sinfulness have said, "If we're really that bad, why didn't God just wipe it all out and start over?" There's only one answer to that question: God's nature, which is love. Thus, every time we look at the Cross we see into the heart of God, and we see a love that would *not* let us go.

But it is not a love based in mushy sentimentalism. It is a love based in God's justice and even His anger, that sin would pervert the original design and purpose of all creation.

JUSTICE AND MERCY

In the Cross the love of God operates to express both justice and mercy. Justice is served in that sin cannot go unpunished. So God offered His only Son in our place to be "a perfect or complete sin offering" (Wesley, *Explanatory Notes*). Mercy is shown in that not only do we not have to bear the full consequences of our sin, but also we are saved from eternal death by Christ's death.

The Cross shatters once and for all any notion that God is against us, unconcerned about us, or absent from us. On the contrary, God stepped into human history to demonstrate His love and to offer each of us an alternative to sin and death.

It is God's cosmic love revealed in the Cross that gives me the basis to believe He loves me personally and specifically. Because of the Cross no one need ever live one day without having the knowledge of being loved—for time and eternity.

3. *The Atonement properly distinguishes the character of Christ.* In a real sense all aspects of Jesus' life and work are focused in the Cross. His prophetic ministry gave rise to the Cross. His priestly ministry was exemplified in the cross. And His kingly ministry was foreshadowed at the Cross.

Wesley used these same three aspects of Christ's ministry in discussing the Cross. He wrote, "We are by nature at a distance from God, alienated from Him, and incapable of a free access to Him. Hence we want a mediator, and intercessor, in a word, a Christ in His priestly office. We find a total darkness, blindness, ignorance of God, and the things of God. Now here we want Christ in His prophetic office, to enlighten our minds, and teach us the whole will of God. We find also within us a strange misrule of appetites and passions. For those we want Christ in His royal character, to reign in our hearts, and subdue all things to Himself" (*Explanatory Notes*).

### ONCE AND FOR ALL

In the Cross God acted decisively once and for all to deal with the problem of sin. The Atonement does not ever have to be repeated. Through the Cross saving grace has been offered. God can never do anything more than He has already done to provide for our salvation. In this historic event we can see the *objective* dimension of the Atonement.

As long as the message of the Cross remains, no one need ever wonder if he can be saved. No one need ever wonder if Christ is the Savior of the world.

4. *The Atonement properly distinguishes the character of the Christian religion.* It is a life and walk of faith. Here the *subjective* dimension of the Atonement is seen. The merits of Christ's death are effective only when appropriated. Dr. Paul Mickey has said it well, "Christ provides but does not unconditionally guarantee salvation. Each person chooses to reject or accept Him and His work" (*Essentials of Wesleyan Theology*).

Unfortunately, some have misunderstood Wesley on this point. They feel he spoke for too great a degree of human freedom in man's response to God's grace. But Wesley stated clearly that even our ability to respond is a gift of grace. Nevertheless, the subjective dimension of the Atonement— our acceptance of it—is essential if we are to be saved.

Having accepted the salvation offered by God in Christ, we then express the second dimension of Christianity: proper works. Christ's death has become the means of our salvation; Christ's life has become the pattern.

Dr. Howard Slaate has correctly called this Wesley's "radical ethic of divine grace" (*Fire in the Brand*). By this Slaate means that no one can accept the merits of the Cross for salvation without also accepting the mandate of the Cross for discipleship. The Atonement is by nature a call to morality and service.

As long as one cross stands atop even one church, we are reminded to proclaim the centrality of the Cross. We can know that faith *in* Christ is the basis of the Christian religion. Faith *for* Christ is the expression of it.

5. *The Atonement properly distinguishes the promise of everlasting life.* The Cross not only is related to the past and present, but also to the future. John Wesley said he wanted to "know one thing—the way to heaven" (*Works*). He believed that in the Cross that way was revealed. He called the Cross "the earnest [guarantee] of life eternal" (*Works*).

Here is where Wesley's theology of Atonement and the kingdom converge. Through Christ's death the new covenant is established and the kingdom is *now*. But the full implications of our salvation and full realization of the kingdom must await a later time. Thus, the kingdom includes the *already* and the *not yet* in Wesley's theology. The Cross represents both dimensions.

SUB-CHRISTIAN THEOLOGY

But the good news is that the Cross stands in the present as a guarantee that "in Christ" all the promises and experiences of eternal life will be realized. Because of the Cross, we can know everlasting life is real.

As far as Wesley's theology is concerned, the Atonement is of central importance. But most importantly we must remember that the message of the Atonement is still central for the Church. We must continue to proclaim the Cross of Christ as the means of salvation for every person. Any church or theology which minimizes the Atonement is at best sub-Christian and at worst un-Christian.

The Cross remains the "distinguishing point" for Christians

in the Wesleyan tradition—indeed for all Christians, only by keeping the Cross central are we true to the Wesleyan spirit. Only by continuing to preach "Christ and Him crucified" will we remember why Christ died in the first place. And only by continuing to lift high the Cross will we offer a dying world its means of salvation.

---

**Steve Harper** is professor of spiritual formation and Wesley studies at Asbury Theological Seminary. He received the Ph.D. from Duke University, where he concentrated in Wesley studies.

His published works include *John Wesley's Message for Today, Devotional Life in the Wesleyan Tradition, Embrace the Spirit* and *God's Call to Excellence.* An elder in the Northwest Texas Annual Conference, Dr. Harper has been a pastor and evangelist and continues to speak frequently at conferences, retreats, and seminars.

## STUDY GUIDE

1. What did Wesley believe to be "the distinguishing point between deism and Christianity"?
2. Identify some reasons why modern man finds it difficult to understand how the Cross can affect us today?
3. What does the Cross tell us about the state of humanity?
4. The author writes, "God takes no delight in needless sacrifice." If true, what does this statement indicate about the meaning and significance of the Cross?

5. Consider the statement, "Every time we look at the cross we see into the heart of God." What does the Cross tell us about the nature of God?
6. Read Hebrews 5:8-9 and Philippians 2:8-9. What do these verses tell us about the character of Jesus Christ? What did bearing the cross mean for Him? What do these verses mean for us today?
7. What does the author mean by "the subjective dimension of the Atonement"? What is its objective dimension?
8. Explain Wesley's radical ethic of divine grace.
9. How does the Cross have significance for our past? For our future?
10. In what sense is the Cross "the earnest (guarantee) of eternal life"?

# 7

# Saved by Faith, Saved by Works, or Why Be Saved at All?

by
James V. Heidinger II

"**I** believe that if I'm active in the church, give regularly, and do my best to help folks in need, God will surely accept me as His child."

"I believe that if I acknowledge my sin, cast myself totally upon God's mercy, and believe in Jesus as Lord, I am assured of a place in Heaven."

"I believe this world is a testing ground for all sorts of people. A loving God wouldn't keep anyone from going to Heaven. Ultimately, all persons will be saved."

On any given Sunday one could hear all of the above sentiments in many of our United Methodist churches. A broad diversity exists among us, even on such crucial issues of our faith. Some would say we're saved by works, others by faith, and some would question whether personal salvation is even a valid concern.

46

*Saved by Faith, Saved by Works, or Why Be Saved at All?*

For historic Reformational Christianity, however, the doctrine of *justification by faith* has always been unquestionably at the center of Christian doctrine.

It was certainly stressed in John Wesley's preaching. His conversion experience at Aldersgate came as he heard someone read from Luther's *Preface to the Book of Romans* which dwells on justification by faith.

How faithful are we United Methodists today in following our Wesleyan doctrinal heritage?

Many United Methodist leaders, including professors at our denominational seminaries, embrace a doctrine of *universalism* these days. That is, they conclude that all persons will eventually be saved. God will allow no one to be eternally separated from Himself. In fact, they would say *everyone* is a child of God—some just don't know it yet. So, the issue of salvation really doesn't matter. How we live here and now is what's important.

Several years ago I preached a sermon on justification by faith to a typical United Methodist congregation. At the end of the sermon, during a talk-back session, I asked whether anyone remembered ever hearing a sermon on that subject. Not a single person lifted a hand.

The memory of that experience still stuns me as I wonder why this central doctrine is so little known or preached. Justification by faith is often unknown, while works-righteousness and universalism are accepted beliefs.

### THE MEANING OF JUSTIFICATION

The doctrine of justification provides the answer to one of mankind's most ancient questions: "How then can man be righteous before God?" (Job 25:4).

A vital concern for every person should be the matter of how to get into a right relationship with God. How can persons overcome the estrangement and alienation that exists between themselves and God?

The Biblical answer to these questions is *justification*. Paul wrote: "Therefore, since we are justified by faith, we have peace with God through our Lord Jesus Christ" (Romans 5:1). "They are justified by his grace as a gift, through the redemption which is in Christ Jesus" (Romans 3:24).

The word *justify* is a legal term and is the opposite of condemn. While to condemn means to declare one guilty, to justify means to declare one innocent, acquitted, righteous, or not guilty.

That is a major reason why the Gospel is "Good News." For through our faith in Christ, God not only forgives, He also justifies. Our sins are not only blotted out, but we are declared righteous in the sight of God.

This means that the person who is justified by faith is actually without guilt in God's eyes. As someone has said, "I'm justified and it is just-as-if-I'd-never-sinned."

## More Than Pardoned

Justification is more than pardon, though. By the life and death of Christ, the demands of God's law have been fully satisfied. God didn't just decide one day that mankind's rebellion doesn't matter after all. Instead, by Jesus' sinless life and obedience He fulfilled the law, satisfying its demands. In His death on the cross, Christ bore the guilt and punishment of all humanity (Isaiah 53:5, 11; II Corinthians 5:21; Galatians 3:13).

So, in justification the very righteousness of Christ is reckoned or attributed to the believer's credit. As Paul wrote, "To one who does not work but trusts Him who justifies the ungodly, his faith is reckoned as righteousness" (Romans 4:5). As one person put it, "The believer's guilt is laid on Christ and Christ's merit is laid on the believer."

Wesley caught the fulness of the meaning of justification when he said:

> The plain Scriptural notion of justification is pardon, the forgiveness of sins. . . To him that is justified or forgiven, God "will not impute sin" to his condemnation. He will not condemn him on that account, either in this

> world, or in that which is to come. . . God will not inflict
> on that sinner what he deserved to suffer, because the Son
> of his love hath suffered for him (Sermon V, "Justification
> by Faith").

This great Biblical truth has been at the heart of Methodist preaching from its beginning. Methodists preached that justification is instantaneous. The moment a person truly believes on the Lord Jesus Christ he is justified—declared not guilty and accounted as righteous.

Even if the believer serves the Lord for 60 years and dies a martyr's death, he can never be "more justified" than at that hour he first believed. For sure, he will be more holy in heart and life, more Christ-like in character, but when one is "not guilty" he cannot be more "not guilty."

Wesley stressed the instantaneous aspect of justification in his sermon, "The Lord Our Righteousness": "But when is the righteousness imputed? When they believe. In that hour the righteousness of Christ is theirs. It is imputed to everyone that believes, as soon as he believes" (Sermon XX).

Justification by faith is central to Christianity. It is little wonder that Luther said this truth is ". . . the principal article of all Christian doctrine, wherein the knowledge of all godliness consisteth. . . If the article of justification be once lost, then is all true Christian doctrine lost" (Luther, *Commentary on the Epistle to the Galatians*).

### THE PROBLEM OF WORKS-RIGHTEOUSNESS

The power of this doctrine of justification by faith is this: It demolishes works-righteousness. It insists that one is forgiven and declared righteous purely by God's grace and not because of one's own merits or personal efforts. Such teaching strikes at nearly every false religious system.

Deep within the human consciousness is the conviction that by doing certain good deeds one can earn credit before God. This thinking says, "Surely God can't be too displeased with me in light of the things I'm doing."

John R.W. Stott calls this belief the religion of the ordinary man in the street. Stott writes, "Indeed, it is the fundamental principle of every religious and moral system in the world except New Testament Christianity. It is popular because it is flattering. It tells a man that if he will only pull his socks up a bit higher and try a bit harder, he will succeed in winning his own salvation" (*The Message of Galatians*, p. 62).

The great delusion many people must overcome is the unfounded belief that one's own religious activity can earn God's favor. The Jews entertained that delusion by taking great pride in their meticulous observance of the law. We entertain the same delusion today when we think our church member-ship, religious heritage, tithing, serving on church committees, faithful church attendance, or other activities can earn us merit in God's sight.

The New Testament clearly teaches that forgiveness comes only through Christ's merit, not our own. When some Jews in the early church began teaching that circumcision was necessary in addition to faith in Christ, Paul adamantly refuted them. He was intolerant—that's right, intolerant—of works-righteousness. He opposed any additions to Biblical faith.

Sadly, much of what goes by the name of "Christian religion" in our modern world is often just human self-assertion in religious disguise. It may have a host of similarities to authentic Christianity and even exist in the environment of a Christian community. But at its core it is still just works-righteousness.

### THE PLACE OF WORKS

One of the great contributions of the Wesleyan revival was its right emphasis on works as the *fruit* of real, Biblical faith. While denying that works had merit in earning God's grace, still Wesley taught vigorously that works are the inevitable fruit of living faith.

He believed that where Christ was dwelling, personal transformation would follow. Works of love and service would flow. And they did—in one of the most remarkable eras of social transformation any generation has ever seen. For Wesley knew of no holiness but *social* holiness.

But the key to Wesley's teaching is that he kept the right relationship between justification and works. He preached that nothing we do ever makes us morally fit to receive justifying faith.

In this teaching Wesley is entirely consistent with our United Methodist Articles of Religion on "Good Works."

> Although good works, which are the fruits of faith, and follow after justification, cannot put away our sins, and endure the severity of God's judgment; yet are they pleasing and acceptable to God in Christ, and spring out of a true and lively faith, insomuch that by them a lively faith may be as evidently known as a tree is discerned by its fruit (Article X, *The Book of Discipline*, p. 57).

For Christians who understand the seriousness of sin, the experience of justification unlocks amazing energy for moral and social good. Such "amazing grace" leaves one overwhelmed and filled with gratitude, as echoed in the songwriter's words, "Love so amazing, so divine, demands my soul, my life, my all."

RECOVERING THE TRUTH

Why, then, is so little attention given to this great theme today? If justification by faith is not being preached from our pulpits, we must ask, "Why not?" Has sentimentalism obscured the seriousness of sin and judgment? Has theological pluralism allowed United Methodists to adjust their understanding of the Christian faith to make it more acceptable to "modern man?"

Let's remember the Gospel has faced opposition in nearly every age. When Luther began preaching that persons are justified before God by faith and not by works, he encountered violent resistance.

Soon he heard the news of the first Protestant martyrs. Several monks had read his work, had turned to his way of thinking, and were burned alive in the Grand Palace in Brussels.

51

When Luther first heard about it he began to pace the floor, saying, "I can't go on. I can't do it anymore. Because of me other men are being killed." But as he wrestled and prayed, he decided he would go on. He understood that because justification by faith was the truth of the Bible, he must go on proclaiming it, no matter what the cost.

The result was the Protestant Reformation. It changed the course of history.

After 200 years of Methodism in America, we need a new reformation. It could happen, if we were truly to rediscover the great New Testament theme of justification by faith.

---

**James V. Heidinger II** is executive secretary/editor of Good News, a position he has held since 1981. His articles and editorials appear regularly in *Good News* magazine, and he is the author of *United Methodist Renewal: What Will It Take?*

Dr. Heidinger is an elder in the East Ohio Annual Conference, where he pastored for 12 years and participated in many conference activities including the conference boards of Discipleship and Ordained Ministry as well as the Bishop's Task Force on Organization and Structure. He is a graduate of Asbury Theological Seminary and received the Doctor of Ministry degree from Wesley Theological Seminary.

## STUDY GUIDE

1. How would you respond to the claim that all persons will eventually be saved? Is every person a child of God? (See John 1:12, John 8:32ff, and II Corinthians 5:18.)

2. What has been your understanding of the doctrine of justification by faith prior to this study? Has this doctrine been a central theme in your Christian experience? Why or why not?

3. Compose your own brief working-definition for justification by faith.

4. In what way is justification more than a pardon? What does the believer have credited to his spiritual and moral account?

5. Early Methodists preached that justification was "instantaneous." In what way is this true?

6. "Though a Christian will be more holy and Christ-like in heart and life after years of being in the faith, he cannot be more justified." Do you agree with this statement? Why or why not?

7. John Stott refers to the "religion of the ordinary man in the street." What does Stott mean? How does justification by faith deal with that kind of religion?

8. The Apostle Paul was intolerant of works-righteousness. (See Galatians 3; Romans 4.) Why was he so adamant about it?

9. Discuss how good works fit into Wesley's scheme of salvation. How important were good works to him? How might Wesley respond to United Methodism's social-action efforts today?

10. Discuss the impact of Luther's discovery of the great New Testament truth that justification is by faith. What impact might it have upon us if we were to rediscover this great doctrine today?

# 8

## Nobody's Perfect, Right?

### *What Wesley Taught About Christian Perfection*

by
William B. Coker

J ohn Wesley referred to the doctrine of Christian perfection as *"the grand depositum* which God has lodged with the people called Methodists." Some have called it "Wesley's heresy."

The difficulty is with the word *perfection.* Understood as the state of being without fault or defect (according to Webster), the term is one that can only be applied truthfully to God.

When Wesley used the term *perfection* to describe a state of grace possible for fallen humanity, it was more than most could accept. In fact, it was more than Wesley himself could allow. So he modified it by explaining that the perfection he preached is not *absolute* perfection, or *angelic* perfection, or *sinless* perfection; rather, it is *Christian* perfection. Still, many remain uncomfortable with the word.

So why use it? Why not abandon it for some better, less antagonizing term? Because, for Wesley, the word is Scriptural. "Therefore," he wrote in 1763, "neither you nor I can in conscience object against it, unless we would send the Holy Ghost to school, and teach Him to speak who made the tongue." Also, the Church has had no qualms about using the word in its liturgy. We pray, "Cleanse the thoughts of our hearts by the inspiration of thy Holy Spirit, that we may *perfectly* love thee. . . ."

Nonetheless, Wesley did use other terms to speak of this work, such as *perfect love, entire sanctification*, and *holiness*. Whatever the term, Wesley's teaching emphasized a state of grace beyond justification or the new birth.

It is a level of Christian experience made possible first, by discovering the depths of carnality in the human heart through the convincing ministry of the Holy Spirit. It is an experience received by the gift of faith through which one believes for the purifying of the heart as a benefit of Christ's atonement. It is the possibility and the privilege of grace extended to every child of God.

### Unrealistic?

Surely, many object, this Wesleyan teaching is unrealistic. Only in the "perfection of burial" (as Calvin would say), only in the holiness of heaven can we be free from carnality!

Much of today's fundamentalism or evangelicalism is adamant about the unresolved depravity of human nature in this life. And what these theologies have to say about holiness can be understood in terms of *unobtainable* pursuits. Anyone claiming to have found the grace of God to achieve such a state is either spiritually naive or guilty of spiritual pride.

But for all of the protests, Wesley's teaching continues to call us back to what the Scripture plainly declares: Jesus told His disciples to "be perfect, as your heavenly Father is perfect" (Matthew 5:48). The promise of the new covenant is "I will sprinkle clean water on you, and you will be clean; I will cleanse you from *all* your filthiness" (Ezekiel 36:25). The standard that God set for His people in both the Old and New

Testaments is "be holy, for I am holy" (Leviticus 11:44; I Peter 1:16).

In his *Plain Account of Christian Perfection* Wesley outlined the spiritual results which characterize this experience:
- purity of intention, dedicating all life to God;
- all the mind which was in Christ, enabling us to walk as Christ walked;
- the circumcision of the heart from all filthiness, all inward as well as outward pollution;
- a renewal of the heart in the whole image of God, the full likeness of Him that created it;
- loving God with all our heart, and our neighbors as ourselves.

To those who take issue with such a standard, Wesley declared that this doctrine was not his. "It is the doctrine of St. Paul, the doctrine of St. James, of St. Peter, and St. John . . . I tell you, as plain as I can speak, where and when I found this. I found it in the oracles of God, in the Old and New Testaments; when I read them with no other view or desire but to save my own soul" (*Plain Account*).

The experience of Christian perfection, as Wesley understood it, was not simultaneous with the new birth, though he agreed there is nothing in the Bible which precludes that. In every person claiming such a state of grace whom he had interviewed, the experience was subsequent to the experience of salvation.

Only having been reconciled to God through Christ "do they see the ground of their heart, which God would not disclose unto them, lest the soul should fail before Him" (*Plain Account*). Psychologically and spiritually, the new birth seems to be a prerequisite for this deeper working of the Holy Spirit.

To understand Wesley's teaching at least three factors must be clearly perceived. The first is that Wesley agrees with Luther and Calvin that the problem of inbred sin, or carnality, remains in the born again Christian. But he disagrees that the child of God must remain a carnal Christian until death.

Believers may, in fact, not avail themselves of the provisions of grace and may not be entirely sanctified until death. Nevertheless, sanctification before death is not only possible but ought to be sought.

## SEEK IT NOW

Christ died to accomplish our sanctification (Ephesians 5:25-27). He prayed that it might be done (John 17:17-23). The Apostle Paul likewise prayed that it might be so (I Thessalonians 5:23). And the Bible teaches that it may be received through faith (Acts 26:18). Since these things are clearly established, one should seek it now.

A second factor is that this subsequent experience which Wesley called entire sanctification or Christian perfection is a gradual process, usually over a number of years, culminating in an instantaneous cleansing. Though Wesley never tried to prescribe how God must effect His work in the human heart, he did not believe in assembly-line saints or instant perfection. Both the new birth and Christian perfection involve the process of divine/human interaction.

A third factor is that Wesley's understanding of Christian perfection is a matter of the heart and not of the humanity. He used the Scriptural metaphor of the *circumcision of the heart* and spoke of perfection in terms of love and intention.

He conceived of no state of grace in which the effects of man's fallenness in terms of knowledge or judgment or emotions would be eradicated. In speaking of those whose hearts had been circumcised by grace Wesley said, "Even these souls dwell in a shattered body, and are so pressed down thereby, that they cannot exert themselves as they would, by thinking, speaking, and acting precisely right" (*Plain Account*).

## IGNORANCE AND MISTAKES

Because there is no cleansing from ignorance, mistakes, and the infirmities of the flesh, those whose hearts are made perfect in love continually need Christ as their High Priest. Though

Wesley differentiated between mistakes and "sin rightly so called," he believed that all transgressions of God's holiness need atonement. Therefore, even the perfect must pray for themselves, "Forgive us our trespasses."

Furthermore, because perfect love is not *absolute* perfect love, it should "abound still more and more in real knowledge and all discernment" (Philippians 1:9). Such growth and development, Wesley anticipated, will continue into eternity.

The question remains: Did Wesley allow his idealism to obscure his perception of reality? Did this "man of one Book" develop a theology of Christian experience which is not "according to the book"?

I find three crucial areas in which Wesley speaks to my need in harmony with God's revealed truth. The first is in the matter of sin. That which separates us from God and hides His face from us (Isaiah 59:1-2) is both a matter of our actions and of the disposition of our hearts. In my case, as I expect is true of all of us, the Holy Spirit first confronted me with my sinful acts. Then it was not until I had repented of my sins and had been brought into a personal relationship with Christ that I began to understand the real problem lay much deeper.

Bishop R.S. Foster described such an awakening in his book *Christian Purity*. Speaking of one genuinely converted he wrote: "But at length a new occasion for disquiet arises. The purified spiritual vision discovers a great depth of iniquity within; and the quickened and tender conscience is convicted of and pained by deep, inwrought pollution." As Bill Bright and Campus Crusade acknowledged, the "Four Spiritual Laws" must have a sequel in "The Spirit-filled Life" if we are to be more than carnal Christians.

## Idle Words

Many of God's people have discovered that His promise to "forgive our sins and cleanse us from all unrighteousness" (I John 1:9) is more than idle words. Clean hands and pure hearts are still the Biblical standard.

A second Wesleyan emphasis which I find to be thoroughly Scriptural is that of holiness. It sounds impressively humble to disclaim holiness as a present reality and to affirm one's unending quest for such a state of grace. But an unbiased reading of the Bible will reveal that God's commands and promises for holiness are not wistful words about the sweet by and by. God clearly instructed Israel that they were to be a holy people.

Paul told the Thessalonians he was anxious to return to their city that he might supply what was lacking in their faith. He prayed that the Lord would "establish [their] hearts unblamable in holiness before our God and Father" (I Thessalonians 3:13).

Peter instructed the temporary residents of the Dispersion to whom he was writing that they were not to "be conformed to [their] former lusts," but rather they were to "be holy . . . in all [their] behavior" as the One who had called them is holy (I Peter 1:14, 15). In spite of all arguments of our unworthiness, holiness is not only God's expectation for His people, it is His expressly commanded purpose. And that in the context of our humanity!

God's standard for holiness is demanding, for sure. Some Christians have even described it so loftily that it is beyond reality. But perhaps we should ask whether our portrayal of an unreal, angelic sanctity might not be a camouflage for second-rate commitment and third-rate spiritual disciplines.

The third Scriptural emphasis for which I am indebted to Wesley is that of Christian perfection. Wesley cannot be ignored when he points out that the term is Biblical. Even our attempts to translate the idea as "maturity" do not cover the Biblical occurrences. What version reads, "Be mature as your Father in heaven is mature"?

## WITHOUT DEFECT

Our problem is that we are functioning with a philosophical definition of perfection, that is, "without flaw or defect," when in truth such a definition does not fit the Biblical usage. The idea of "completeness" more adequately interprets Scriptural use. That is why Wesley could say that all he meant by Christian perfection is "to love God with all one's heart, mind, soul, and strength."

Wesley's plan for the Methodist societies was to thrust the newly converted Christians immediately into the quest for wholeness of heart—to assist them to believe that God *could* and to pray that God *would* cleanse their hearts so they might perfectly love Him. Then, if by faith they came into the blessing of a pure heart, they were to understand that only by a moment-by-moment relationship with their Lord, living in complete dependence upon His grace, could they be sustained in such a holy oneness.

Who is to say that such a Biblical standard of grace is not really possible? The founder of Methodism certainly believed that it is.

---

**William B. Coker** is the senior pastor of World Gospel Mission Church in Terre Haute, Indiana. He pastored United Methodist churches in Louisiana, Mississippi, Kentucky, and North Indiana before beginning an academic career which included teaching Bible and Biblical languages at Asbury College and later serving as the college's vice-president and academic dean. He also served as vice-president for mission advancement at OMS International.

Dr. Coker has contributed articles to *The Zondervan Pictorial Encyclopedia of the Bible, Beacon Dictionary of Theology, Hebrew Abstracts,* and *Theological Wordbook of the Old Testament.* He is a graduate of Tulane University and Asbury Theological Seminary and received the Ph.D. from Hebrew Union College.

STUDY GUIDE

1. What questions arise within you when you think of the word "perfection"? Do you agree that "Christian perfection" is a term worth keeping and using, or does it create confusion?

2. Have you heard much teaching concerning, or thought much about Wesley's phrase "going on to perfection"? What does it mean to you?

3. The author lists some of the results of Christian perfection that Wesley outlined in his classic, *A Plain Account of Christian Perfection*. Are these results unobtainable? Or are they a "possibility and privilege of God's grace"? Discuss.

4. Review the three factors the author mentions as necessary for understanding Wesley's teaching on Christian perfection. The second factor mentions "a gradual process . . . culminating in an instantaneous cleansing." Are both the "gradual" and "instantaneous" aspects necessary ingredients to Christian perfection? Why or why not?

5. If Christian perfection deals with love and intention, does that leave any room for errors in knowledge or judgment?

6. Normally, does a sinner under conviction for his sinful acts have an adequate understanding of the deeper issue of the sin nature? What have you learned about the sin nature since finding Christ as your personal Savior?

7. We often hear the holy life portrayed as an unreal, angelic sanctity. Might this portrayal be, as the author suggests, a camouflage for "second-rate commitment and third-rate spiritual disciplines"? Discuss.

8. Could Christian perfection be as simple as "to love God with all one's heart, mind, soul, and strength"? If I am not "going on to perfection" as described here, then what am I doing?

9. Is the author of this chapter writing about a moment by moment relationship or a once-for-all experience? Does it matter?

10. What would be some indicators that one has experienced "perfect love"?

# 9

# I Will Build My Church

## *What Wesley Taught About the Church*

by

Frank Bateman Stanger

**H**ow would John Wesley react if he could see the Methodist Church of today?

I spoke recently to a group of preachers in a western state. After explaining about this article I was to write, I asked them to discuss with me how they thought Wesley would react to contemporary Methodism. During each of the following five days I met with a different group of ministers as well as with lay people. And on numerous occasions this same issue was discussed. Some of the reflections from those group sessions, along with my own studied observations, will be incorporated in this article.

The question, however, is not easy to answer for several reasons. First, John Wesley is not living in our highly industrialized, institutionalized society. We do not know how he would react to it all and what would be his approach to such a cultural setting.

Moreover, it is so easy for contemporary Methodists to read into Wesley their own particular perspectives and viewpoints. For example, some believe Wesley was an evangelical purist; others are sure he was an evangelical pluralist.

In spite of these difficulties, we are at least aware of the basic theological, ethical, and ecclesiastical principles which undergirded Wesley's ministry in his day. And it is logical to assume they would have been his guiding principles in any generation.

Wesley's view of the Church was shaped in large part by his upbringing. From the earliest days of his childhood he was under the religious influence of the Church of England. He grew up in the traditions and practices of the Established Church.

His father, Samuel Wesley, was an ordained priest of the Church of England. He served as the rector of Epworth Parish in Lincolnshire for nearly 40 years. John's mother, Susanna Wesley, was the daughter of Samuel Annesley, a dissenting minister and one of many who suffered under the cruel law of non-conformity. But at the early age of 13 Susanna deliberately conformed to the Church of England, leaving the dissenters.

The education of the Wesley children was entrusted almost entirely to Susanna. She was particularly concerned about their religious training. She prepared for them an admirably clear body of explanation regarding the catechism and the creed. She met with each child separately once a week at a specified time for an hour of religious conversation and instruction.

John Wesley lived his entire childhood in this religious environment, and his dominant spiritual influence was that of the Church of England. He was truly a son of the Church.

With that background in mind, let me be presumptuous, perhaps, in asking: "Was Wesley in some spiritual areas a casualty of his Church?" Did the Established Church with its neglect of personal spiritual experience and its deistic theological presuppositions impede, in some instances, Wesley's quest for inward holiness? Did the Church thwart him in the fulfillment of his spiritual desires?

It can be inferred that the Established Church alone would never have led him to Aldersgate. Rather, it was the traditional doctrine of the Church, illumined and quickened by pietistic insights into personal spiritual experience, that made possible Wesley's transformation at Aldersgate.

May 24, 1738, was the date of that Aldersgate experience. John Faulkner writes of Wesley's passionate commitment to the Church of England up to the time of Aldersgate:

It is acknowledged on all hands that previous to his conversion in 1738 Wesley was an ardent High Churchman. He recommended confession, he practiced weekly communion, he observed all the festivals and the fasts on Wednesdays and Fridays, he mixed the sacramental wine with water, and in other respects anticipated the churchly enthusiasm of the Oxford reformers of 1833 (*Wesley as Sociologist, Theologian, Churchman*).

### EFFECTS OF ALDERSGATE

But Faulkner writes in equally decisive words about the effects of Wesley's Aldersgate experience upon his theology of the Church:

That experience cut up Wesley's High Church theology by the roots—I mean in its essential features. No longer was the stress to be laid upon the sacraments, upon observances and rites as means of salvation, but solely upon faith; and the chief means of conversion was preaching, not baptism nor confirmation nor catechizing nor worship. From this all the important features of the Methodist revival followed as a matter of course: (1) the organization of the converted into societies and classes, (2) the employment of lay preachers, (3) extemporaneous prayer in the divine service.

As the Methodist movement spread, Wesley's loyalty to the Church of England on the one hand and his innovations in church practices on the other showed both a *conservatism* and a *radicalism*. He maintained his old love for the church of his youth and strove constantly to keep his preachers and members in as close touch with it as he could. But he ruthlessly departed from such conservatism whenever he thought it necessary for the spiritual vitality of his movement.

Faulkner concludes:

> From a study of all the facts, it is readily seen that it is impossible to form a consistent picture of Wesley's churchmanship. It is crossed through and through with contradictions. His feelings, early training, all his associations, his prejudices, some of his principles, led him to warm regard for the church of his father and mother. The whole drift of his life after 1738 and all the crucial steps of his movement led him in effect to radical separation from it, accompanied at times with stern denunciation of it, and a formal repudiation of all its laws except the rubrics in its ritual, which also were thrown to the wind in his ordinations.

We must also raise the issue which Frank Baker discusses in his book, *John Wesley and the Church of England*. Is there room for an intensely evangelical revivalistic movement in an established church? Unless a denomination is willing to get rid of its "old bottles" in order to contain "new wine," is not separation ultimately inevitable?

All of this is relevant to today's church. Who causes polarization within a church body? Is it those who would recall the church to its traditional heritage, or those who refuse to be sensitive and responsive to such recall?

### MARKS OF THE CHURCH

John Wesley accepted the statement about the nature of the Church as contained in the Thirty-Nine Articles of Religion of the Church of England. Article XIX declares: "The visible Church of Christ is a congregation of faithful men in which the pure Word of God is preached, and the sacraments duly administered according to Christ's ordinance, in all those things that of necessity are requisite to the same."

Wesley accepted the traditional marks of the Church:

*The Church is one*. He continually affirmed his stand against division and schism.

*The Church is holy*. The holiness of the Church has a two-fold foundation: it is the Church of the Holy Spirit and the true members of the Church are holy.

*The Church is apostolic.* Wesley clung to the Church of England because of its attachment to the doctrines and practices of the apostolic church.

*The Church is universal.* Wherever there are believers in Jesus Christ, regardless of place or race, there the Church exists. Wesley wrote: "The Catholic or universal Church is all the persons in the universe whom God hath so called out of the world as to entitle them to be 'one body,' united by 'one spirit,' having one faith, one hope, one baptism; one God and Father of all. . ." (*Sermons,* "Of the Church").

Wesley's concept of the Church was always colored by two considerations: (1) The Church is a community of believers who have experienced salvation in Jesus Christ. (2) The Church is always in mission.

In Wesley's sermon "Of the Church" he makes it clear that the Church is not characterized by a common creed or the holding of identical opinions. Neither is the Church universal designated by a liturgical orthodoxy, by the proper administration of the sacraments. Rather, the Church is a universal body of believers filled with and united by the Holy Spirit. Without the unifying, creative, and sustaining work of the Holy Spirit there could be no Church.

The second consideration for Wesley is that the Church is always in mission. That mission is the salvation of the world. Christian conversion is the end for which the Church is the means.

But what about Wesley's reaction to contemporary Methodism? I believe Wesley would be pleased with many things that are happening in Methodist churches today. He would welcome the renaissance of evangelical theology and the quickened interest in Bible study and Biblical preaching. He would be favorably inclined toward the observance of the bicentennial of American Methodism, and especially in those attempts to rediscover our theological roots.

I assume that Wesley would welcome all our Methodist talk about evangelism, even to the setting of greatly increased membership goals. But he would insist that there be more than talk—that Methodists become evangelists throughout the nation and seek to win the unsaved to Christ.

I am confident that Wesley would be gratified by the widespread interest in the person and ministry of the Holy Spirit, and that he would add his full weight to all that is being done in the area of spiritual formation.

Wesley would be glad to see the widespread interest in social issues and the attempt to reform society through the Gospel of Jesus Christ. Alongside this he would certainly be approving of those who seek to revitalize missionary evangelism which seeks the salvation of persons in all the world, which is always the "Methodist parish."

But honestly, are there things in contemporary Methodism that would be appalling to Mr. Wesley? Let's face the fact that the dominant peril facing the United Methodist Church is indiscriminate and unrestrained pluralism. We are rapidly becoming a church where just about anything goes. Here is where John Wesley would vigorously wave a red flag and command Methodism to turn around in its tracks.

Wesley undoubtedly would not be too disturbed by a pluralism in ecclesiastical structures and in forms of worship. But he would have nothing to do with either theological or ethical pluralism. He insisted upon the "core doctrines" of the Christian faith. His "order of salvation" is universally applicable.

### The Holy Life

Wesley's insistence upon the holy life is the direct opposite of the popular tendency. This trend permits even Christians to express themselves in whatever ethical patterns and lifestyles seem to provide the greatest freedom for potential growth. Modern Methodism needs to recover both the meaning and manifestation of the holy life, modeled after the teachings of the Holy Scripture and interpreted so aptly by Mr. Wesley.

Contemporary Methodism needs to rediscover the nature of Christian discipleship as expressed through disciplined living. Early Methodist societies were disciplined colonies of believers. Often in his *Journal* Wesley wrote, "I disciplined the society." Just suppose Wesley would discipline Methodist churches today—what would be left? The results would certainly be a discouraging start for the '84 General Conference's goal to double UM membership by the close of this century.

John Wesley would be profoundly concerned about the spiritual vitality of the church. In his "Thoughts Upon Methodism," he wrote in 1768:

> I am not afraid that the people called Methodists should ever cease to exist either in Europe or America; but I am afraid lest they should only exist as a dead sect, having the form of religion without the power. And this undoubtedly will be the case unless they hold fast both the doctrine, spirit, and discipline with which they first set out.

How would John Wesley react to recent stories carried in United Methodist publications? You answer that question as you imagine John Wesley reading such items as these:

"Religious Leaders Say That Tobacco Is not a Moral Issue." "Bishop to Speak at Conference-wide Rally of Gay Christians." "Period of Thanksgiving Engaged in Because Quotas Have Been Surpassed in Election of Bishops." "Increasing Numbers of Ministers Reject Doctrine of Virgin Birth and Bodily Resurrection of Christ as Theologically Essential." "Annual Conference Seeks to Have 1984 General Conference Legislation Against Ordination of Homosexuals Declared Unconstitutional by Judicial Council." "Board of Trustees at Denominational School Refuse to Take Further Action Against Drinking On Campus." "Redemption Must Be Viewed Primarily in Relation to Society."

How would John Wesley react? You be the judge.

But as you decide, remember the Wesley who was a son of the Church, a priest of the Church, a servant of the Church, and a catalyst for the renewal of the Church. Keep in mind that he would always judge out of total dedication to and love for the Church, and because of an undying concern for and unbridled optimism about the future of the Church.

---

**Frank Bateman Stanger (1914 - 1986)** was for 20 years the president of Asbury Theological Seminary. He was a member of the Southern New Jersey Annual Conference and pastored churches there from 1935-1959.

Dr. Stanger frequently wrote for United Methodist curriculum materials and published many books including *The Gifts of the Spirit, He Healed Them,* and *God's Healing Community.* His academic degrees are from Asbury College, A.B.; Princeton Theological Seminary, Th.B.; and Temple University, S.T.M., S.T.D.

## STUDY GUIDE

1. Is it possible to know precisely what Wesley would think of the United Methodist Church today? Why or why not?
2. How did Wesley's conversion change his view of the church?
3. After Aldersgate, how did Wesley respond when positions taken by the Church of England came into conflict with the essentials of his faith?

4. When a reform-minded person challenges a denomination today, what principles should he/she employ?
5. Can an established church ever welcome a true reformer? Why or why not?
6. What "traditional marks of the Church" did Wesley accept?
7. Do true churches all have to believe the same doctrines?
8. What would Wesley likely think of "theological pluralism"?
9. What was Wesley afraid might someday happen to "the people called Methodists"? Discuss.
10. How do you think Wesley would respond to this headline: "Increasing Numbers of Ministers Reject Doctrines of Virgin Birth and Bodily Resurrection of Christ"? Why? What do *you* think of the headline?

# 10

# Wesley's Principle for Social Action

by
Frank Baker

**D**uring this century there has been an increased emphasis upon the social dimension of Methodist witness. In 1908, inspired by a theology of the social gospel proclaimed by the Baptist, Walter Rauschenbusch, the Methodist Episcopal Church set forth the Methodist Social Creed. It became the nucleus for a similar statement adopted by the Federal Council of Churches.

More recently our brothers and sisters in Latin America have extended this approach still further. In their liberation theology they seek to remove both the dependence of the poor upon the rich and of Christian theology itself upon those who are economically comfortable. They have begun to search the writings of John Wesley for support—and with considerable success.

True, it is unthinkable that Wesley would have echoed in his day the revolutionary demands of the liberationist. True, he seems never to have used the phrase "social gospel" though he did speak approvingly of "social religion" and "knows of no religion but social; no holiness but social holiness" (preface to *Hymns and Sacred Poems*).

Wesley's constant emphasis upon the dangers of riches makes many of us in a wealthy society very uncomfortable. Yet, even more intense than his condemnation of luxurious living and unconsecrated wealth is his passionate concern for the poor. Wesley demonstrated this concern primarily in various forms of Christian philanthropy rather than in social reforms. He seems to have regarded social service as a more natural and inevitable outflow of Christian love than using the somewhat tainted weapon of politics.

Yet there can be no doubt that Wesley's social practices were the necessary outcome of his social principles, that his philanthropy sprang from his theology. It all began with the New Testament, of course. The Lord Jesus Christ had taught Wesley to say, "Our Father." And the fatherhood of God implied the brotherhood of man. Wesley's favorite epistle challenged him, "that the one who loves God should love his brother also" (I John 4:21). And Wesley's comment on this verse carefully defined the term "brother" as "everyone, whatever his opinions or mode of worship be, purely because he is the child and bears the image of God. Bigotry is properly the want of this pure and universal love."

Our Lord's two great commands were to love God and to love your neighbor—the latter defined by the parable of the Good Samaritan as *anyone in need.* In 18th-century England the distinctions between rich and poor were as outrageously visible as in first-century Palestine, and one's most needy neighbors were obviously the poor.

The coin of Christianity was two-sided for Wesley and was meant to be spent in two ways: in securing and maintaining personal salvation and in serving one's neighbors. Both separately and jointly these formed the unity of living to the

73

glory of God, of doing God's will. Charles Wesley captured this duality of the Christian calling as he paraphrased Matthew Henry's comment on Leviticus 8:35:

> *A charge to keep I have,*
> *A God to glorify,*
> *A never-dying soul to save,*
> *And fit it for the sky;*
> *To serve the present age,*
> *My calling to fulfill;*
> *O may it all my powers engage*
> *To do my Master's will.*

For a time John Wesley toyed with the idea of a separated Christian community modeled on early Christian communism—when "all those who had believed were together, and had all things in common." His comment on Acts 2:45 exclaims wistfully: "It was a natural fruit of that love wherewith each member of the community loved every other as his own soul. And if the whole Christian Church had continued in this spirit, this usage must have continued through all ages." Wesley never quite forsook this dream. And during his last three decades he encouraged "The Community" formed by his followers for social service in London.

Soon after the development of his United Societies in 1739, however, he deliberately set aside any plans to organize Methodist monastics. He maintained in one of his sermons on the Sermon on the Mount, that "Christianity is essentially a social religion, and that to turn it into a solitary religion is indeed to destroy it." He realized that we must come to terms with the society in which we live, with all its faults.

In turn this implied dealing seriously with the problem of money—gaining it, saving it, and spending it, as good stewards exercising one's stewardship to the glory of God. Speaking of Wesley's "radical rejection of surplus accumulation," Dr. Albert Outler claims: "On no other single point, save only faith and holy living, is Wesley more insistent, consistent—and out of step with the bourgeois spirit of his age" (*The Bicentennial Edition of the Works of John Wesley*, Vol. 2).

DO GOOD UNTO ALL MEN

Thus, Methodism's ministry to society was, in Wesley's view, inseparable from the preaching of salvation by faith. And he sought to make this clear in the major documents in which he introduced his societies to a skeptical and often antagonistic public. In *The Character of a Methodist* (1742) he stated that a Methodist was not distinguised from others by peculiar opinions, words and phrases, customs, or even by the proclamation of salvation by faith alone.

"A Methodist" Wesley claimed, "is one who has the love of God shed abroad in his heart by the Holy Ghost given unto him, one who loves the Lord his God with all his heart, and with all his soul, and with all his mind, and with all his strength" (section 5). After expounding the spiritual implications of this (largely from I Thessalonians 5:16-18), Wesley continues:

> And while he thus always exercises his love to God by prayer without ceasing, rejoicing evermore, and in everything giving thanks, this commandment is written in his heart, that "he that loveth God, loves his brother also." And he accordingly "loves his neighbour as himself;" he loves every man as his own soul (section 9).

A year later Wesley took the same Methodist social principles which he had thus announced to the general public, and summarized them as *General Rules* for his own people. Although he claimed there was only one condition for Methodist membership, "a desire . . . to be saved from their sins," he insisted that for continuance in the society this must be confirmed by steady behavior befitting such a desire: avoiding evil, doing good, and attending upon all the ordinances of God. Wesley provided an all-embracing understanding of "doing good":

> By doing good . . . as they (Christians) have opportunity . . . of every possible sort and as far as is possible to all men:
>
> To their bodies, of the ability which God giveth, by giving food to the hungry, by clothing the naked, by visiting or helping them that are sick, or in prison.
>
> To their souls, by instructing, reproving, or exhorting all they have any intercourse with. . . .

For Wesley the most *immediate* thing (whether or not it was in the long run the most important) was caring for bodily needs —there was no point in making even the most eloquent evangelical appeal to a starving man!

### SEND RELIEF TO THE POOR

Wesley's *Plain Account of the People Called Methodists* (1749) was again roughly divided into halves, the first devoted to spiritual principles and practices, the second to the social. He showed how the Methodist social principles were being worked out in practice, usually with an eye to similar precedents in the early Christian church.

The essential function of his stewards, for example, was "to send relief to the poor" with the added rule: "Give none that asks relief either an ill word or an ill look. Do not hurt them, if you cannot help." Soon the stewards found it difficult to keep in touch with all the sick, especially since none of these ministries were confined to Methodists only. At a general meeting of his London society, therefore, Wesley called for voluntary "sick visitors" and sent them out by couples into 23 divisions of the city.

Medical care for the poor then forced itself upon Wesley's attention, and he "thought of a kind of desperate expedient," and began the first free clinic and dispensary in London. He also sponsored a poorhouse (financing it by faith), in which he housed "nine widows, two poor children, two upper servants, a maid and a man," as well as a school both for basic education, for spiritual training, and for reaching the parents. Another venture which was of immense social assistance was Wesley's "lending fund" from which he was able to rescue some people from debtors' prisons, and to set others up in honest work. He appealed for financial aid to this cause by an adaptation of a line by George Herbert: "Join hands with God to make a poor man live."

This varied social ministry was not unique to Methodism, but it was characteristic. And several of Wesley's social ventures were pioneering experiments of great value. None of these, or his later developments, formed a blueprint for saving society.

Wesley believed in the leading of the Holy Spirit as he pursued the call to serve his contemporaries. He had no carefully thought-out scheme for social renewal, no political program for Methodism. Nevertheless, he did also urge the honest, diligent, and caring exercise of voting, upon the minority who possessed that privilege. And he was ready to cooperate with other influential leaders, even in the world of politics.

Wesley's most noteworthy effort in this field was his lifelong campaign, first, to improve the lot of the black slave, and then to banish from the earth what he called "the execrable villainy" of slavery itself, "the scandal of religion . . . and of human nature" (Letter to William Wilberforce, Feb. 24, 1791). Even on his deathbed, because Wesley loved the God whom he was going to meet, he continued to love his brothers and sisters also.

---

**Frank Baker** is the emeritus professor of English church history at Duke Divinity School. Born in Kingston-upon-Hull, England, Dr. Baker pastored Methodist churches in Great Britain for 25 years, and earned his Ph.D. from Nottingham University, before emigrating to the United States in 1960. He has written or edited over 300 articles and 18 books; some notable works are *John Wesley and the Church of England; From Wesley to Asbury: Studies in Early American Methodism;* and the first two volumes of Wesley's *Letters* for the bicentennial *Works* project. In 1969, Dr. Baker was honored with the St. George's Gold Medal for distinguished service to the United Methodist Church.

## STUDY GUIDE

1. Consider the familiar phrase of John Wesley that he "knows of no religion but social; no holiness but social holiness." What does he mean?

2. A key to understanding Wesley is to realize that he had a "passionate concern for the poor." Do you? Does your church? If not, discuss the reasons why this concern is not as strong as it might be. What does the Scripture say concerning the poor? (See Isaiah 1; Amos 2; 2 Corinthians 9; Romans 16:26.)

3. The author refers to Wesley's two-sided coin: (1) maintaining personal salvation and (2) serving one's neighbors. "Both separately and jointly these formed the unity of living to the glory of God, of doing God's will." How do you see this unity expressed in your church today? Is there balance?

4. Discuss Wesley's words about money, "Gain all you can, save all you can, give all you can" as well as his "radical rejection of surplus accumulation." Are these principles relevant for today's more sophisticated society?

5. Some people suggest there is division between those United Methodists who believe in social action versus those who believe in personal faith. What do you believe are the real issues in regard to social action that divide United Methodists?

6. As you read of Wesley's ministries to the poor, including a free clinic, a dispensary, a poorhouse, schools for basic education, and a "lending fund," what becomes clear about Wesley's commitment to helping the poor? Yet, the

author notes he had "no scheme for social renewal, no political program for Methodism." Discuss.

7. Wesley was, however, ready to cooperate with other influential leaders, even in the world of politics. How does Wesley's view of the political world compare with that of the United Methodist Church today? What are the dangers, if any, of too close a linkage between the Church and the political world?

8. One often hears the phrase, "You can't legislate morality." How do you respond to that phrase? How did Wesley respond? To this claim, some have responded, "Yes, but you can use legislation to help protect the poor from exploitation." Discuss.

9. Consider the *balance* of Wesley the evangelist and winner of souls with Wesley the reformer whose social consciousness helped save England from a violent revolution. Why is this kind of balance, this full-orbed kind of ministry, difficult to attain?

10. What do you question most about today's forms of social action? What can you affirm most?

# 11

# The Lord's Supper in the Wesleyan Tradition

by
John R. Tyson

**I**t is difficult to imagine any single change that has distanced modern United Methodism from the Methodism of John and Charles Wesley more than our approach to the Lord's Supper. Part of this distancing results from the way in which American Methodism owed its rapid growth to the evangelization of the expanding frontier.

On the frontier Methodists had no choice but to celebrate the Lord's Supper sporadically, because of the relatively small number of circuit-riding preachers who followed the pioneers westward. But these days are not those; and today we can, if we are willing to learn from the Wesleys, recover something that is essential and distinctive about our United Methodist heritage.

It is clear that our present practice of quarterly Communion does not square with John Wesley's direction for the American Methodists. In fact, his letter of instruction (September 10,

1784) marked out quite a different course: "I also desire the Elders to administer the Supper of the Lord on *every* Lord's Day."

John also wrote a sermon on the Lord's Supper in 1732 titled, "The Duty of Constant Communion." And he published a shortened version of it near the end of his life. Wesley wanted the sermon to "show that it is the duty of every Christian to receive the Lord's Supper *as often as he can.* . ." In this "duty," as in most others that he urged upon his followers, Wesley practiced what he preached. One author, who did a statistical survey of John Wesley's written records, concluded that Wesley took the Lord's Supper on the average of once every four or five days (John Bowmer, *The Lord's Supper in Early Methodism*).

In 1745 the Wesleys published the most complete statement of their theology of this sacrament. *Hymns on the Lord's Supper (HLS)* included their condensed version of a eucharistic handbook by Dr. Brevint, plus 155 hymns composed by the Wesleys themselves. The book was a best-seller in the Wesleys' lifetime, running through nine successive editions.

John and Charles divided this collection of hymns into six basic sections, which spell out the nature and focus of the Lord's Supper. The six section headings describe the main features of a Wesleyan understanding of the Lord's Supper:

1. As it is a memorial of the sufferings and death of Christ
2. As it is a sign and a means of grace
3. The sacrament as a pledge of heaven
4. As it implies a sacrifice
5. Concerning the sacrifice of our persons
6. After the sacrament

### As it is a Memorial of the Sufferings and Death of Christ

To say that the Lord's Supper is a "memorial" is to follow the words of Jesus, who said, "do this in remembrance of Me" (I Corinthians 11:24). In so doing we focus our attention through the "sign" (in creatures of bread and wine) to the thing signified, the reconciling death of Christ. In Wesleyan terms, however, "memorial" means more than merely a remembrance of Christ's death. Time and space are no barriers to this sacramental memorial. It crosses those dimensions which separate us from Calvary in order to set Christ's death in the midst of the congregation, and to demand of us repentance as well as faith:

> *Hearts of stone, relent, relent*
> *Break by Jesu's Cross subdued,*
> *See His body mangled, rent,*
> *. . . Sinful soul, what hast thou done?*
> *Murther'd God's eternal Son! (HLS, #23).*

This memorial is also more than a "calling to mind." It is a "setting before my eyes" that bridges the distance between past and present by communicating, in the vibrant language of religious experience, the effectiveness of Christ's death:

> *O what a soul-transporting feast*
> *Doth this communion yield!*
> *Remembering here Thy Passion past,*
> *We with Thy Love are filled (HLS, #94).*

Quite a bit of ink has been spilled trying to decide exactly how the Wesleys conceived of Christ's presence in the sacrament or the elements of bread and wine. The hymns voice an unwillingness to breach this mystery by definition. Instead they point to the beneficial results of Christ's presence in the Lord's Supper:

> *How He did these creatures raise,*
> *And make this bread and wine*
> *Organs to convey His grace*
> *To this poor soul of mine,*
> *I cannot the way decry,*
> *Need not know the mystery;*
> *Was blind, but now I see (HLS, #258).*

Charles attacked the idea that Christ is *physically* localized in the Communion elements. But Charles would not say that

Christ was absent from the sacrament, since Christ Himself set forth these "means" as vehicles of His love:

> *No local Deity*
> *We worship, Lord, in Thee:*
> *Free Thy grace and unconfined,*
> *Yet it here doth freest move,*
> *In the means Thy love enjoined*
> *Look we for Thy richest love* (*HLS*, #63).

Thus, the Lord's Supper is Christ's "choicest instrument" which "doth all His blessings give" (*HLS*, #42).

To describe how Christ's healing presence is communicated through the sacrament, Charles turned to the account of Jesus healing a woman with a hemorrhage through the instrument of His garment:

> *Sinner, with awe draw near,*
> *And find Thy Saviour here,*
> *In His ordinances still,*
> *Touch His sacramental clothes;*
> *Present in His power to heal,*
> *Virtue from His body flows* (*HLS*, #39).

Christ is present in the sacrament not by virtue of His physical location in or around the elements, but by the power of the Holy Spirit—whose task it is to bear witness to Christ and bring Him to remembrance (John 15:26):

> *Come Holy Ghost, Thine influence shed,*
> *And realize the sign;*
> *Thy life infuse into the bread,*
> *Thy power into the wine.*
> *Effectual let the tokens prove,*
> *And made, by heavenly art,*
> *Fit channels to convey Thy love*
> *To every faithful heart* (*HLS*, #72).

Just as outward eating fills and refreshes the inner person, so also "eating through faith" brings "the fulness of Christ" into the life of the Christian through the sacrament.

## As it is a Sign and a Means of Grace

The Wesleys believed that the sacraments were windows through which God's grace shone into human hearts. Standing on the foundation of Scripture and Church tradition, John wrote: "the whole body of Christians being agreed, that Christ had ordained certain outward means for conveying his grace into the souls of men" (*Works*, Vol. V, p. 185). He followed St. Augustine and The *Anglican Articles of Religion* in defining a sacrament as "an outward sign of an inward grace, and a means whereby we receive the same" (*Works*, Vol. V, p. 186).

The "outward sign" refers to the elements of bread and wine which serve as "channels" or "instruments" which funnel "an inward grace" into the life of the Church. This "inward grace" is nothing less than "all the benefits of Christ," which John Wesley typically classified as "preventing, justifying, or sanctifying grace" (*Works*, Vol. V, p. 187).

To identify the "preventing" grace in the sacrament is to say that it has the power to convict and lead people to faith in Christ. To say that "justifying" grace is communicated through the Lord's Supper is to say that it can be a channel of God's saving power. And to view Communion as an instrument of "sanctifying grace" is to indicate that Communion is one of the ways God leads his people "on to perfection" by purging out their sin and sinful attitudes and growing His love within them.

In a similar way, John Wesley's "preface" to *Hymns on the Lord's Supper* described the brothers' understanding of the sacrament in three important verbs: "represent," "convey," and "assure." The sacrament functioned to (1) "represent the sufferings of Christ which are past. . . ," (2) "convey the first-fruits of these sufferings in present graces, whereof it is a means," and (3) "assure us of glory to come whereof it is an infallible pledge."

John's *Standard Sermon #16*, "On the Means of Grace," made it clear that he intended to steer a course between those who "abused" the Lord's Supper by making it into a form of works-righteousness and those who "despised" the sacrament by neglecting it altogether. For the Wesleys to term the Lord's Supper "a sign and means of grace" was to say that it was a symbol *and* an instrument of God's redemptive power, which both "shows" and "bestows" the grace of our Lord:

> *The sacred, true, effectual sign,*
> *Thy body and Thy blood it shows;*
> *The glorious instrument Divine*
> *Thy mercy and Thy strength bestows*
> *We see the blood that seals our peace,*
> *Thy pardoning mercy we receive:*
> *The bread doth visibly express*
> *The strength through which our spirits live*
> *(HLS, #28).*

### THE SACRAMENT AS A PLEDGE OF HEAVEN

For the Wesleys to term the Lord's Supper "a pledge of heaven" was to focus our attention on the restorative power of God's grace. The fellowship with Christ and Christians in sacramental meal is like a piece of heaven broken off above, shaped into a tangible promise of life with God, and placed in our midst:

> *We feel the earnest in our hearts!*
> *Of our eternal rest (HLS, #97)*

or

> *How glorious is the life above,*
> *Which in this ordinance we taste;*
> *That fullness of celestial love,*
> *That joy which shall forever last (HLS, #90).*

The eucharistic fellowship at the Lord's table is a *foretaste* of the glory which one day will become a *full taste* when "this perishable will have put on the imperishable, and this mortal will have put on immortality" (I Corinthians 15:51 ff). This *foretaste* is a part of the path to perfection which brings the power of the heavenly kingdom among us, as Charles asked:

> *Where shall this memorial end?*
> *Thither let our souls ascend,*
> *Live on earth to heaven restored,*
> *Wait the coming of the Lord (HLS, #98).*

It is as though the Lord's Supper is a moment when the windows of heaven are thrown open wide and as we look in, full of anticipation, a dazzling ray of heavenly light shoots forth to flood and transform our inward lives:

> *The light of life eternal darts,*
> *Into our souls a dazzling ray,*
> *A drop of heaven o'erflows our hearts*
> *and deluges the house of clay (HLS, #90).*

### As It Implies a Sacrifice

The Lord's Supper sets the sacrificial death of Christ before the eyes and hearts of the people of God. When Jesus said "this is my body," and "this is My blood of the covenant, which is poured out for many for forgiveness of sins" (Matthew 26:26ff), He identified the sacramental meal as an emblem of His own death. In Charles Wesley's poetic imagination the cross of Calvary becomes transposed upon the Church's altar:

> *The cross on Calvary He bore,*
> *He suffer'd once to die no more,*
> *But left a sacred pledqe behind:*
> *See here!—It on Thy altar lies,*
> *A memorial of the sacrifice*
> *He offer'd once for all mankind (HLS, #121).*

To call Jesus' death a "sacrifice" is to draw attention to His role as Redeemer to recognize that His was a death for the forgiveness (atonement) of sins, a death which He died not for Himself but for all of us:

> *All hail, Redeemer of mankind!*
> *Thy life on Calvary resign'd*
> *Did fully once for all atone;*
> *Thy blood hath paid our utmost price*

> *Thine all-sufficient sacrifice*
> *. . .The sacrifice is all complete (HLS, #124).*

### CONCERNING THE SACRIFICE OF OUR PERSONS

Just as the Lord's Supper points to Christ's sacrificial giving of Himself on our behalf, so also does a Wesleyan approach to the sacrament demand that we understand it as an act through which Christians give themselves to Christ. This act of utter consecration results in a renewal that touches every facet of a person's life. As Charles Wesley prayed through his eucharistic hymn:

> *Take my soul and body's powers,*
> *Take my memory, mind, and will,*
> *All my goods and all my hours,*
> *All I know, and all I feel,*
> *All I think, and speak and do;*
> *Take my heart—but make it new (HLS, #155).*

### AFTER THE SACRAMENT

The Wesleys' eucharistic manual, *Hymns on the Lord's Supper,* closed with seven short hymns designed to remind believers that as we leave the Lord's table we do not leave His presence. These hymns are full of the joy and adoration which flow into the Christian's life after having met Christ through His supper. The hymns dismiss us from the Lord's table invigorated with the power for Christian living:

> *O, let Thy wondrous mercy's praise*
> *Inspire and consecrate my lays [plans]*
> *And take up all my lines and life;*
> *Thy praise my every breath employ;*
> *Be all my business, all my joy (HLS, #160).*

The Wesleys left their spiritual descendents a rich sacramental heritage. The brothers' fervor for the Lord's Supper was not based on sheer formalism or born in a threadbare sense of religious tradition. Rather, they embraced the sacrament because it both "shows" (as a sign) and "bestows" (as a means)

God's grace. It communicates to us the benefits of Christ's death and resurrection, and demands we respond to Him in faith and commitment of our entire selves. John Wesley enumerated these benefits as "preventing" (convicting), "justifying" (converting), and "sanctifying" (confirming) *grace*.

Today, the sacrament of the Lord's Supper is too often neglected. We still need to participate in Christ's reconciling ministry through the means of grace. Nowhere will United Methodists be more *united* than in communion with Christ and one another around the Lord's table. Nor shall we be in full possession of our vital heritage as Methodists until we turn with renewed vigor toward the life-changing power flowing through the Lord's Supper. John Wesley still urges us across the ages, "Let all . . . who truly desire the grace of God, eat of that bread, and drink of that cup."

---

**John R. Tyson** is professor of theology at Houghton College. He received the Ph.D. from Drew University where, for his doctoral dissertation, he did research on Charles Wesley's theology of the Cross.

Dr. Tyson speaks and writes about the Wesleys, their hymns and the Wesleyan heritage. He has written articles for such publications as *The Methodist Quarterly Review* and *Evangelical Quarterly,* and has authored two books, *Charles Wesley: A Reader* and *Charles Wesley On Sanctification.*

## STUDY GUIDE

1. In John Wesley's letter of instruction to American Methodists, he instructed the elders to serve the Lord's Supper (Communion) how often? How often did John Wesley himself take the Lord's Supper?

2. How often do you celebrate the Lord's Supper? Do you sense a need to take Communion more or less often than you do now? Why?

3. In what sense is the Lord's Supper "a memorial of the sufferings and death of Christ"? Discuss.

4. How did the Wesleys solve the "mystery" of *how* Christ is present in the sacrament of Communion or the elements of bread and wine?

5. What did the Wesleys mean when they referred to the Lord's Supper as "a sign and a means of grace"?

6. According to the Wesleys, the "benefits of Christ" which come through the Lord's Supper include "preventing, justifying, and sanctifying grace." What did the Wesleys mean by each of these three aspects of grace?

7. What *two* "sacrifices" are symbolized and implied by the sacrament of Communion?

8. According to John Wesley, how was the sacrament of Communion "abused" by some in his day? How was it "despised"?

9. Review the six main features of a Wesleyan understanding of the Lord's Supper. In your own words give a brief explanation of each feature.

10. Identify at least one insight gleaned from this chapter that increases your appreciation for the sacrament of Communion.

# 12

# Ready For His Return

## *What Wesley Taught About End Times*

by
Joel B. Green

"**P**reaching in the evening at Spitalfields on 'Prepare to meet thy God,' I largely showed the utter absurdity of the supposition that the world was to end that night. But notwithstanding all I could say, many were afraid to go to bed, and some wandered about in the fields, being persuaded that, if the world did not end, at least London would be swallowed up by an earthquake. I went to bed at my usual time, and was fast asleep by ten o'clock."

As illustrated by this journal entry above, John Wesley was not one to predict dates for the end times. Yet that is not to say he was uninterested in the second coming of Christ or eternal life.

In fact, it is not an overexaggeration to say that for Wesley *everything* is oriented to the fulfillment of God's rule in the coming kingdom. But the kingdom is no "pie-in-the-sky-in-the-sweet-by-and-by." It is a reality which calls for present, radical commitment—a life of Christian holiness and service under the present reign of Christ.

### THE KINGDOM NOW AND THEN

The Old Testament depicts God's kingdom as the ideal existence where all men and women live under the reign of their Lord. The prophets expressed their hope in a new world, where God's rule would be extended universally—a time of peace and justice under God which would never end (Isaiah 2:4; Daniel 7:14; Zechariah 14:9).

In our own time the nature of the kingdom of God, especially as presented in the New Testament, has been a matter of controversy. Some have insisted that, for Jesus and the authors of the New Testament, the kingdom is a *present reality*. And they are right—partially. Jesus did teach that in His person and work the kingdom had invaded history (Matthew 12:22-28). Likewise, early Christianity proclaimed the present reign, or lordship, of Jesus Christ.

Wesley, too, spoke of "that kingdom of God upon earth whereunto all true believers in Christ, all real Christians, belong" ("Christian Perfection"). Life with God is not merely something to which we may look forward.

> Eternal life commences, when it pleases the Father to reveal his Son in our hearts; when we first know Christ . . . then it is that heaven is opened in the soul, that the proper, heavenly state commences, while the love of God, as loving us, is shed abroad in the heart, instantly producing love to all mankind ("Spiritual Worship").

In an important sense, then, the kingdom of God is a present reality.

But others have urged, with equal justification, that God's reign will be *realized in the future*. According to the Gospels, Jesus looked for the kingdom to be fulfilled in the future. (See, for example, Matthew 7:21-23 and the parables about the kingdom.) The early Christians anticipated the fulfillment of the kingdom at Jesus' return (Revelation 11:15).

As strongly as Wesley emphasized the present experience of life with God, he was equally confident that the kingdom was "not yet." In a sermon based on Revelation 21:5—"Behold, I make all things new"—he underscored the *future* dimensions of God's kingdom:

> Very many commentators entertain a strange opinion, that this relates only to the present state of things; and gravely tell us that the words are to be referred to the flourishing state of the Church which commenced after the heathen persecutions. . . . What a miserable way is this of making void the whole counsel of God, with regard to all that grand chain of events, in reference to his Church, yea, and to all mankind, from the time that John was in Patmos, unto the end of the world! ("The New Creation").

The kingdom may be present, but it is also future. Can both be right, we may ask. Can the rule of God be both "present" and "not yet"? Yes! We experience a foretaste of the kingdom now, and yet long for its fulfillment when Jesus returns.

In his time, Wesley recognized this dual nature of God's reign, and in his *Explanatory Notes upon the New Testament* wrote:

> The kingdom of heaven and the kingdom of God are but two phrases for the same thing. They mean, not barely a future happy state in heaven, but a state to be enjoyed on earth. . . . In some places of Scripture the phrase more particularly denotes the state of it on earth; in others, it signifies only the state of glory; but it generally includes both (on Matthew 3:2).

## THE LAST DAY

What will happen at the end, when Christ returns to establish His kingdom? Wesley often spoke of "that day"—that is, the final Day of the Lord. He thought of it in terms of three related events: (1) the general resurrection, (2) the final judgment, and (3) the new creation.

When Wesley taught on the *general resurrection*, he encouraged believers to "maintain [the resurrection] hope in its full energy; longing for that glorious day, when, in the utmost extent of the expression, *death shall be swallowed up* forever, and millions of voices, after the long silence of the grave, shall burst out at once into that triumphant song, *O death, where is thy sting? O hades, where is thy victory?"* (*Explanatory Notes upon the New Testament*, on I Corinthians 15:55). At the resurrection we will be raised in glory, to receive new bodies—immortal and incorruptible.

Afterwards will come *the judgment* when the righteous will be separated from the unrighteous. At that time everything will be revealed—every appetite, inclination, affection, disposition: "So shall it be clearly and infallibly seen, who was righteous, and who was unrighteous; and in what degree every action or person or character was either good or evil" ("The Great Assize"). The end of this judgment is that the righteous will inherit eternal life and the unrighteous will be delivered into everlasting punishment.

What qualifies a person for eternal life?

> None shall live with God, but he that now lives to God; none shall enjoy the glory of God in heaven, but that he bears the image of God on earth; none that is not saved from sin here can be saved from hell hereafter; none can see the kingdom of God above, unless the kingdom of God be in him below. Whosoever will reign with God in heaven, must have Christ reigning in him on earth ("A Blow at the Root; or Christ Stabbed in the House of His Friends").

This view of judgment and eternal life is fully consistent with Wesley's emphasis on personal holiness, on living out one's salvation by growing in Christ-likeness. For Wesley, the end times must never be divorced from life in the here and now.

At last, however, *all will be made new*—and Wesley accentuates the "all." Not only humanity, but "the whole brute creation will then, undoubtedly, be restored, not only to the vigour, strength, and swiftness which they had at their creation, but to a higher degree . . . [as high] as the understanding of an elephant is beyond that of a worm" ("The Great Deliverance").

But the most glorious transformation will be that of men and women, as the effects of sin are nullified and God's people are fully restored. Then there will be no more pain, no more suffering, no more death, and no more sin. "Hence will arise an unmixed state of holiness and happiness, far superior to that which Adam enjoyed in Paradise" ("The New Creation").

When will all this take place, and what will be the sign of its coming? On this matter Wesley differed sharply from those who major on end-time speculation, in his day as in our own. In outlining his understanding of Christian perfection, he noted that Christians are never perfect in knowledge, and that our ignorance extends to the time of the Last Day.

We can be certain of the return of Christ and the consummation of the kingdom. But our certainty should not be the basis for speculation. Whatever the Bible does reveal about the end times, this knowledge is not given to tickle our ears or satisfy our curiosity, but to call us to a right response now. "Therefore, beloved, since you look to [a new heaven and a new earth], be diligent to be found by Him in peace, spotless and blameless" (ll Peter 3:14).

Wesley recognized that, in view of the coming kingdom and kingdom come, Scriptural Christianity calls for radical commitment . . . *now!*

### THE DEMANDS OF THE KINGDOM

This present obedience, Wesley believed, should include two elements. First, he emphasized *present commitment and devotion.* In his sermon on "The Signs of the Times," Wesley taught that, if we want to be ready for the Day of the Lord, we must "begin at the root . . . Now repent, and believe the Gospel!" Then, "Stir up the gift of God that is within you. Walk in the light, as he is in the light." Having become Christians through repentance and faith, we must *grow in grace and holiness.*

> The righteousness of Christ is doubtless necessary for any
> soul that enters into glory: But so is personal holiness too,
> for every child of man. ("On the Wedding Garment").

But personal commitment and devotion are only part of a right response to the future God has designed. For Wesley, Christianity was "inward religion," but much more. He goes on to give this counsel: "It behooves you, in the next place, to help your neighbors."

Scripture is never optimistic that human efforts will build the kingdom. After all, the kingdom is *God's*, and so He alone can usher it in. Nevertheless, we must prepare for the coming kingdom as we serve the Lord Jesus now.

This service is accomplished on the one hand as we, in Wesley's words, "proclaim the glad tidings of salvation ready to be revealed" On the other hand, "helping your neighbors" means working for social renewal. In Wesley's own ministry this concern was obvious in his efforts on behalf of the poor and imprisoned, and in his spirited denunciation of American slavery.

### LIVING BETWEEN THE TIMES

For now, we live between the first coming of Jesus and His future return, between the institution of the kingdom of God and its consummation. While we long for our future eternal life with God, the completion of our salvation, we can experience a foretaste of that life now as we serve the risen Lord.

———————

**Joel B. Green** is associate professor of New Testament and academic dean at New College for Advanced Christian Studies, in Berkeley, California. A life-long United Methodist, he has ministered in UM churches in the United States as well as the British Methodist Church.

He has authored *How to Read Prophecy* and *Kingdom of*

*God: Its Meaning and Mandate* in addition to numerous articles. Joel is a graduate of Texas Tech University and Perkins School of Theology, and received the Ph.D. from the University of Aberdeen in Scotland.

## STUDY GUIDE

1. Do you recall persons or groups who have predicted dates and places for end-time events? What do you remember about such groups and their predictions? Discuss.
2. In what way is the kingdom of God a present reality that calls for a radical commitment, a life of Christian holiness here and now? What Scripture passages support this view? Discuss.
3. In light of the previous question, can it also be true that the kingdom of God has a future dimension about it? What tensions, both theoretical and practical, are inherent in the view of the kingdom as being both "present" and "not yet"? Discuss.
4. Wesley, along with many others, spoke of the end time as the "day of the Lord" or "that day." Wesley believed that a central event on "that day" would be the general resurrection. Read I Corinthians 15 and several commentaries or reference works to see what you can learn about the general resurrection. Will our bodies be resurrected or just our souls? Discuss.
5. For Wesley, another central event of the end time was the final judgment. Teaching about a clear and final separation is not popular in our era of inclusiveness. Will the unrighteous, in fact, be delivered into everlasting punishment? Check other passages of Scripture and discuss.

6. Wesley's view of the final judgment linked one's eternal fate closely with one's personal holiness and authentic Christian living. Does this imply salvation by works in Wesley's understanding? Discuss.

7. A third central event of the end time for Wesley was the new creation. Read and discuss Romans 8:19 about the whole creation groaning for Christ's redemption.

8. Wesley taught that because of our limited understanding, we should be tentative about the details of the last days. We can be certain, however, about Christ's return and the consummation of the kingdom of God. Are you sure, personally, about the certainty of our Lord's return? Does Scripture support it?

9. Wesley stressed two elements concerning the believers's readiness for the Day of the Lord. The first was present commitment and devotion, including repentance, faith, and walking in the light. The second was the serving of one's neighbors. Is this an adequate statement, in your view? If not, what more do you feel is needed?

10. Wesley believed that Christians live between the times. Christ has come, but He will come again. The kingdom of God has been instituted, but it will be consummated. Eternal life is a present possession of the believer, but still only a foretaste of that which is to come. If we took these truths to heart, how might they affect our living?

# 13

# How Revival Comes

by
Robert E. Coleman

**M**ethodism at heart is a revival movement. When the Spirit of revival does not pervade the church, the body may survive as an institution but it is lifeless. So it was no mere formality when John Wesley asked early Methodists, "What can be done in order to revive the work of God where it is decayed?" (John Wesley, *Works*). At issue was the very reason for their existence. Those early Methodists understood revival in the Biblical sense of "living as God intended." The word *revival* in the Old Testament conveyed the idea of "breathing." "Breath" was the expression of life. So revival was "breathing in the breath of God" (e.g., Ezekiel 37:5,6,14; Job 33:4). The word is also used in the Old Testament to mean "live" "restore" "preserve" "heal" "prosper" or "save."

In the New Testament the word for revival means "to live again" (Revelation 20:5; Romans 14:9). Other words liken revival to the rekindling of a slowly dying fire (II Timothy 1:6) or to a plant putting forth fresh shoots and blooming again (Philippians 4:10).

The basic idea always is *the return of something to its true nature and purpose.* Revival can be seen then as that "sovereign work of God in which He visits His own people, restoring, reanimating, and releasing them in the fulness of His blessings" (Stephen Olford, *Heart-Cry for Revival*).

The most immediate *evidence* of revival is seen in the vitality of individual Christian experience. A person walking after the Spirit knows an unobstructed relationship with God. There is an assurance of sins forgiven; the mind is clean; the soul is free. Deep within the heart comes a song, and praise of the Most High fills life with worship.

To be sure there is still suffering and temptation, but through it all shines the light of Christ. He is Lord! His peace overrides every storm. His victory overcomes the world.

Wesley equated this inner state of revival with "holiness of heart and life," which he believed was "the weight of all religion." Wesley viewed this as a state whereby one lives in "total deadness to the world, and in fervent love to God and man" (John Wesley, *Works*).

By New Testament standards there is nothing unusual about such an experience. It is the way people should always live. Revival simply brings out what it is to be spiritually whole. To use the words of Roy Hession, it is you and I "walking along the highway in complete oneness with the Lord Jesus and with one another, with cups continually cleansed and overflowing with the life and love of God" (*The Calvary Road*).

In this personal sense revival should be a constant experience. The notion that it is a seasonal thing comes from the inconsistency of human nature, not the will of God. Unfortunately, for most of us there come those periods of spiritual sluggishness which make restoration necessary. But if we lived in the continual fulness of the Spirit, as God desires, revival would be an abiding reality.

Revival, however, does not end with mere personal blessing. Invariably, as individuals enter into the life-flow of the Holy Spirit, and this experience is multiplied in the lives of others, the church feels a new unity of faith and purpose. God's people become sensitive to one another's burdens and together seek to fulfill the law of Christ.

### REVIVAL AFFECTS SOCIETY

Not only is a deep love experienced within the fellowship, but revived church members develop concern for the unbelieving persons outside the church. In this way the dynamic for evangelism and social concern is born. Christ's love cannot be self-contained when hearts are full.

Inevitably, society feels the impact. When the Gospel goes forth in power, both in word and in deed, the world takes note that men and women have been with Jesus.

Conviction of sin settles down. Sinners are moved to seek the Savior. Restitution is made. Moral conditions improve. The law is more strictly obeyed. Home life takes on a new glow. Benevolent institutions thrive. Integrity makes its way into government. And if penetration is deep and extensive the whole land may learn justice and righteousness.

Another by-product of revival is *church growth*. The extraordinary growth of early American Methodism offers a prime example. Where the records show large increases in membership, a study of other available information usually reveals that the church was in revival.

One explanation for the early concentration of Methodist strength in Maryland, Delaware, and Virginia is the fact that in those places Methodists were most caught up in a religious awakening. The rapid growth of the new denomination from 1784 to 1790 may be attributed to the same religious fervor. Jesse Lee, one first-hand observer, compared it to "taking the kingdom by violence."

On the other hand, during the years 1793 to 1798, when growth subsided, reports of revival are conspicuously absent from Methodist sources. Not until the Great Awakening at the turn of the 19th century did the church again experience significant growth. And that thrust continued until the decline of the revival spirit as the century advanced.

Revival activity was so intertwined with early Methodist growth that no real distinction was made between evangelistic services and the regular work of the societies. A not uncommon entry in Francis Asbury's *Journal* for September 8, 1789, illustrates this:

> Preached in town and at the Point. The last quarterly meeting was a wonder-working time: fifty or sixty souls, then and there appeared to be brought to God; people were daily praying from house to house; some crying for mercy, others rejoicing in God, and not a few, day after day, joining in society for the benefit of a religious fellowship. Praise the Lord, O my soul!

The intensity of feeling described in such accounts, no doubt, soon subsided. But the matter-of-factness with which they are recalled reflects how Methodists *expected* God to do wondrous things.

More often than not congregations without any clerical direction would feel the moving of the Spirit and start evangelizing on their own. Often the itinerant preacher would arrive at an appointment to discover that revival had already come. It remained for him only to baptize the converts and receive them into church membership.

## REVIVAL NOT PROGRAMS

How wonderful it would be to see this dynamic outreach become commonplace again in Methodism! It would put some action into all the talk today about church growth. Let a church burn with the fire of the Holy Spirit and nothing in the world can restrain a concern for lost souls. Before such holy love principalities of darkness cannot prevent multitudes from storming into the kingdom.

But until the Spirit of God fills us it is unrealistic to believe that He will flow through us. Mere programs and campaigns won't do it, however well intended. If Methodism is to recover her glory then the call must be back to our roots, back to Pentecost, back to true Christian holiness. For where holiness "is little insisted on" as Wesley keenly observed, "there is little increase, either in the number or the growth of the hearers" (John Wesley, *Letters*).

Underlying this concern is the recognition of divine authority. There is no point talking about revival unless we believe that God means business. "If My people who are called by My name humble themselves and pray, and seek My face and turn from their wicked ways, then will I hear from heaven, will forgive their sin, and will heal their land" (II Chronicles 7:14).

A thousand other promises declare the same provision. God is *for* us. But do we really believe what He says?

If we doubt the reliability of His Word there will be little reason to measure our lives by it. Liberal views of Scripture, with their attachment to theological pluralism, will never produce revival.

God has declared that unto Him "every knee will bow," (Isaiah 45:23). It is not our place to dispute or minimize the message. Nor are we to defend what is written. The Bible is not on trial; we are. Our place is to trust and obey. Once this is settled, as it was for Wesley, our hearts are ready for spiritual instruction.

When the Word confronts us with the holy character of God revealed in Jesus Christ we see that our presumed righteousness is really only filthy rags. The props of self-sufficiency are knocked out from under our pride. As the realization of sin grips our hearts the Spirit urges us to repent and throw ourselves on the Lord's mercy.

Anything that hinders the flow of God's grace must go. Unbelief, lust, lying, ingratitude, indifference to responsibility, prayerlessness, disregard of discipline, backbiting, envy, bitterness, deceitfulness, hypocrisy—whatever it is, if it is contrary to the will of God, it must be confessed and forsaken and the cleansing blood of Christ must be appropriated by faith.

This relentless quest for perfection, a distinctive aspect of Methodist thought, allows no compromise with evil. "Speak and spare not," said Wesley. For "till you press the believers to expect full salvation now you must not look for any revival" (John Wesley, *Letters*).

### A Strategy For Today

Near the close of the Conference of Leeds in 1755, someone confronted Wesley with the charge that some of his preachers were not "alive" as they once were. Though the report was disturbing, the patriarch of Methodism would not let his disappointment obscure the more immediate concern. He asked:

> Who of you is exemplary, so much alive to God, so as to carry fire with him wherever you go? Who of you is a pattern of self-denial in little things? Who of you goes through his work willingly and diligently? Is your heart in the work wholly? (John Wesley, *Letters*).

Answering yes to these questions is where revival begins. The time has come to quit complaining about the faults of other people. Regardless of what our position may be in the church and whatever may be our gifts, are the *conditions* for revival being fulfilled in our lives? Are we obedient to the Holy Spirit?

One person aflame with holiness will ignite another. As the divine spark leaps from heart to heart, and more persons seek first the kingdom, the cry for revival will increase.

Look around for these people. Such a group is probably waiting for direction right now in your church. They may be unorganized, perhaps not even aware of your mutual concern, but they are there. And they may only need encouragement and leadership to become a mighty force for revival. Do not worry if your numbers are small. Jesus started with just a handful, too.

Discover what you can do together to stimulate your faith and ministry. One way to help this nucleus develop is to meet regularly for fellowship, Bible study, and prayer. Together you can work out a discipline in light of your needs.

But the group must not become preoccupied with its own interests. The water of life must be kept flowing, or it will become stagnant. So find ways to share God's love to the waiting world.

With the extension of the group's ministry, new people will want to become a part. Other fellowships will emerge. Gradually the growing core of committed disciples will have impact on the larger congregation. Increasing numbers of people will launch out into their spheres of ministry.

The goal is total mobilization of the total church for the total mission. When this commitment is harnessed with the yoke of Christ the whole Body becomes an instrument of revival.

### What Would Wesley Do?

People have often asked me, "If Wesley were a member of the United Methodist Church today, what would he do?" I reply, "He would do the same thing he did when he was in the Church of England in the 18th century. Beginning with himself and a few kindred spirits he would set out by the grace of God 'to raise up a holy people.'"

I do not see him forming a political action lobby to pressure the decadent Anglican Church to change its ways. Wesley was not unmindful of the church's problems; he was simply occupied with higher priorities. Wesley was primarily concerned with revival, real holiness revival. He felt that by expending his energies in this cause his work would have its most enduring value.

We would do well to follow his course. I believe, to paraphrase the words of Wesley, that such a people "who fear nothing but sin and desire nothing but God," though small in number, "whether they be clergymen or laymen, such alone will shake the gates of hell and set up the kingom of heaven upon earth."

**Robert E. Coleman** is a professor of evangelism and the director of the School of World Mission and Evangelism at Trinity Evangelical Divinity School. He has authored 19 books including *The Master Plan of Evangelism,* which recently passed its 50th printing. Translations of one or more of his books are published in 82 languages.

Dr. Coleman's ministry centers on life-style evangelism and discipleship. He is president of Christian Outreach, a service organization committed to discipleship resource development, chairman of the North American Lausanne Committee for World Evangelization, and director of the Billy Graham Institute at Wheaton. He received the Ph.D. from Iowa State University.

## STUDY GUIDE

1. What memories, thoughts, or feelings come to you when you hear the word "revival"? How are your perceptions of revival similar to or different from the author's understanding of revival?
2. According to the author, what is "the most immediate evidence of revival"?
3. How does the author describe the effects of revival in the individual experience of a believer? Have you ever had an experience like or similar to this? Discuss.
4. What is the relationship between revival and social concern?
5. What evidence does the author give to demonstrate that church growth results from revival?
6. In the author's view, what is the relationship between revival and a person's or group's response to Scripture?

7. Describe briefly the author's strategy for reviving the church today. Do you agree with this strategy? What important elements, if any, would you want to add to this strategy?
8. Look back at the definitions you wrote of the six "essential doctrines" (chapter 1), or turn to the list of these doctrines in that chapter. How has this book confirmed or increased your understanding of each of these doctrines?
9. Describe the new insight or perspective gained from reading this book which you value most. Explain why.
10. Identify two or three ideas or emphases presented in this book which you would like to see implemented in your own life or in the life of your church. What, specifically, will you do to see that these ideas are implemented?

# Appendix A

# The Junaluska Affirmation

*Of Scriptural Christianity for United Methodists*

*INTRODUCTION TO JUNALUSKA AFFIRMATION*
*"Methodism's Silent Minority," an article by Charles W. Keysor in the July 14, 1966 issue of the* Christian Advocate *was the beginning of the Good News ministry. This article, prepared in response to the editor's invitation to write about the beliefs of Methodist evangelicals, brought a flood of positive response: evangelical theology was not dead in United Methodism.*

*The mood in the church at the time was secular. Its slogan was: "Let the world set the agenda." Such an approach to theology could hardly be accepted as a modern-day restatement of the theological distinctives of a Wesleyan, Reformed theological tradition. A confusing uncertainty surrounded any public statement by evangelical Methodists about their beliefs. Herein was a theological mandate. In April, 1974 the Good News Board of Directors appointed a "Theology and Doctrine Task Force" to prepare an affirmative statement of Scriptural Christianity for Good News.*

*Dr. Paul A. Mickey, a member of the faculty at the Divinity School at Duke University, was chosen to chair the task force. Other members of the task force included Rev. Riley Case, Rev. Dr. James V. Heidinger II, Rev. Dr. Charles W. Keysor, Rev. Dr. Dennis F. Kinlaw, Mr. Lawrence Souder, Rev. Dr. Frank B. Stanger, and Rev. Dr. Robert Stamps.*

*On July 20, 1975, the statement "An Affirmation of Scriptural Christianity for United Methodists" was adopted by the Board of Directors of Good News during the 1975 Convocation of United Methodists for Evangelical Christianity meeting at Lake Junaluska, North Carolina; hence, the title, "The Junaluska Affirmation."*

#### PREAMBLE

In a time of theological pluralism, Good News and other evangelicals within United Methodism have thought it necessary to reaffirm the historic faith of the Church. Our theological understanding of this faith has been expressed in the Apostles' Creed, Nicene Creed, and in John Wesley's standard *Sermons* and the *Explanatory Notes upon the New Testament*. We affirm in their entirety the validity and integrity of these expressions of Scriptural truth, and recognize them as the doctrinal standards of our denomination.

We also recognize that our situation calls for a contemporary restatement of these truths. The merging of two great traditions, the Evangelical United Brethren and the Methodist, with their two authentic witnesses to the historic faith, *The Confession of Faith* and *The Articles of Religion*, gives further occasion for such a statement. Moreover, we recognize the mandate which the doctrinal statement of the 1972 General Conference has placed upon "all its members to accept the challenge of responsible theological reflection."

Consequently, we offer to the United Methodist Church this theological affirmation of Scriptural Christianity.

### THE HOLY TRINITY

*Scriptural Christianity affirms* the existence of the one Eternal God who has revealed Himself as Father, Son and Holy Spirit, three equal but distinct Persons, mysteriously united in the Godhead which the Church historically has described as the Holy Trinity.

### GOD THE FATHER

*Scriptural Christianity affirms* that the first Person of the Holy Trinity, God the Father, is the Eternal One and reigns supremely. He has provided a covenant through which His creatures can be redeemed and through which His creation will be liberated from all evil and brought to final righteousness at the end of the age.

### GOD THE SON

*Scriptural Christianity affirms* that the second Person of the Holy Trinity, the Eternal Son, became incarnate as Mary's virgin-born Child, Jesus of Nazareth, the Christ. In His unique Person, He revealed to us both the fulness of deity and the fulness of humanity. By His life, suffering, death, resurrection and ascension He provided the only way of salvation. His sacrifice on the cross once for all was to reconcile the Holy God and sinners, thus providing the only way of access to the Father. Now He intercedes as High Priest before the Father, awaiting the day when He will return to judge every person, living and dead, and to consummate His Kingdom.

### GOD THE HOLY SPIRIT

*Scriptural Christianity affirms* that the third Person of the Holy Trinity, the Holy Spirit, was active from the beginning in creation, revelation and redemption. It was through His anointing that prophets received the Word of God, priests became intermediaries between God and His people, and kings were given ruling authority. The Spirit's presence and power, measured in the Old Testament, were found without measure in Jesus of Nazareth, the Anointed. The Spirit convicts and woos the lost, gives new birth to the penitent, and abides in the believer, perfecting holiness and empowering the Church to carry out Christ's mission in the world. He came to indwell His Church at Pentecost, enabling believers to yield fruit and endowing them with spiritual gifts according to His will. He bears witness to Christ and guides God's people into His truth. He inspired the Holy Scriptures, God's written Word, and continues to illuminate His people concerning His will and truth. His guidance is always in harmony with Christ and the truth as given in the Holy Scriptures.

### HUMANITY

*Scriptural Christianity affirms* that man and woman are fashioned in the image of God and are different from all of God's other creatures. God intends that we should glorify Him and enjoy Him forever. Since the Fall of Adam the corruption of sin has pervaded every person and extended into social relationships, societal systems, and all creation. This corruption is so pervasive that we are not capable of positive response to God's offer of redemption, except by the prevenient, or preparing, grace of God. Only through the justifying, regenerating and sanctifying work of the Triune God can we be saved from the corruption of sin, become increasingly conformed to the image of Christ, and restored to the relationships which God has intended for us.

### THE HOLY SCRIPTURES

*Scriptural Christianity affirms* as the only written Word of God the Old and New Testaments. These Holy Scriptures contain all that is necessary for our knowledge of God's holy and sovereign will, of Jesus Christ the only Redeemer, of our salvation, and of our growth in grace. They are to be received through the Holy Spirit as the guide and final authority for the faith and conduct of individuals and the doctrines and life of the Church. Whatever is not clearly revealed in, or plainly established as truth by, the Holy Scriptures cannot be required as an article of faith nor be taught as essential to salvation. Anything contrary to the teachings of the Holy Scriptures is contrary to the purposes of God and must, therefore, be opposed. The authority of Scripture derives from the fact that God, through His Spirit, inspired the authors, causing them to perceive God's truth and record it with accuracy. It is evident that the Holy Scriptures have been preserved during the long process of transmission through copyists and translators, and we attribute such accurate preservation to the work of the Holy Spirit. These Scriptures are supremely authoritative for the Church's teaching, preaching, witness, identifying error, correcting the erring, and training believers for ministry in and through the Church.

## SALVATION

*Scriptural Christianity affirms* that God offers salvation to a sinful humanity and a lost world through Jesus Christ. By His death on the cross the sinless Son propitiated the holy wrath of the Father, a righteous anger occasioned by sin. By His resurrection from the dead, the glorified Son raises us to newness of life. When we appropriate by faith God's atoning work in Jesus Christ we are forgiven, justified, regenerated by His Holy Spirit, and adopted into the family of God. By His grace He sanctifies His children, purifying their hearts by faith, renewing them in the image of God, and enabling them to love God and neighbor with whole heart. The fulness of God's great salvation will come with the return of Christ. This cosmic event will signal the resurrection of the saved to eternal life and the lost to eternal damnation, the liberation of creation from the Adamic curse, God's final victory over every power and dominion, and the establishment of the new heaven and the new earth.

## THE CHURCH

*Scriptural Christianity affirms* that the Church of Jesus Christ is the community of all true believers under His sovereign

Lordship. This Church, the Body of Christ, is *one* because it shares one Lord, one faith, one baptism. It is *holy* because it belongs to God and is set apart for His purposes in the world. It is *apostolic* because it partakes of the authority granted to the apostles by Christ Himself. It is *universal* because it includes all believers, both living and dead, in every nation, regardless of denominational affiliation. Its authenticity is to be found wherever the pure Word of God is preached and taught; wherever the Sacraments of Baptism and Holy Communion are celebrated in obedience to Christ's command; wherever the gifts of the Holy Spirit upbuild the body and bring spiritual growth; wherever the Spirit of God creates a loving, caring fellowship, and a faithfulness in witness and service to the world; and wherever discipline is administered with love under the guidance of the Word of God. The Church, as the Bride of Christ, will ultimately be joined with her Lord in triumphant glory.

ETHICS

*Scriptural Christianity affirms* that we are God's workmanship, created in Christ Jesus for good works. These works are the loving expressions of gratitude by the believer for the new life received in Christ. They do not earn one's salvation nor are they a substitute for God's work of redemption. Rather, they are the result of regeneration and are manifest in the believer as evidence of a living faith.

God has called us to do justice, to love kindness, and to walk humbly with Him. In the Scriptures are found the standards and principles that guide the believer in this walk. These ethical imperatives, willingly accepted by the believer, enable us to be a part of God's purpose in the world. Moreover, in this we are called to an obedience that does not stop short of our willingness to suffer for righteousness' sake, even unto death.

Our life in Christ includes an unstinting devotion to deeds of kindness and mercy and a wholehearted participation in collective efforts to alleviate need and suffering. The believer will work for honesty, justice and equity in human affairs, all of which witness to inherent rights and a basic dignity common to all persons created in the image of God. Such contemporary issues as racism, housing, welfare, education, Marxism, capitalism, hunger, crime, sexism, family relationships, aging, sexuality, drugs and alcohol, abortion, leisure, pornography, and related issues call for prayerful consideration, thoughtful analysis, and appropriate action from Christians, and must always be a matter of concern to the Church. Thus, we remember that faith without works is dead.

# Appendix B

# The Character of a Methodist

by
John Wesley

*Few Methodists today are aware that Methodism's founder wrote a profound definition of the Methodist character. We have preserved the ideas of Wesley but tried to express them in twentieth-century language.* —EDITOR

The distinguishing marks of Methodists are not their opinions of any sort . . . their accepting this or that scheme of religion . . . their embracing any particular set of notions . . . or mouthing the judgments of one person or another. All these are quite wide of the point.

Therefore, whoever imagines that a Methodist is a person of such and such opinion is sadly ignorant. We do believe that "all Scripture is given by inspiration of God." This distinguishes us from all non-Christians. We believe that the written Word of God is the only and sufficient rule both of Christian faith and practice in our lives.

We believe that Christ is the eternal, supreme God. This distinguishes us from those who consider Jesus Christ to be less than divine.

*But as to all opinions which do not strike at the root of Christianity,* we think and let think. This means that whether or not these secondary opinions are right or wrong, they are *not* the distinguishing marks of a Methodist.

Neither are words or phrases of any sort. For our religion does not depend on any peculiar way of speaking. We do not rely upon any quaint or uncommon expressions. The most obvious, easy words which convey the truth most effectively—these we Methodists prefer, in daily speech and when we speak about the things of God. We never depart from the most common, ordinary way of speaking—unless it be to express scriptural truths in the words of Scripture. And we don't suppose any Christian will condemn us for this!

We don't put on airs by repeating certain scriptural expressions—unless these are used by the inspired writers themselves.

Our religion does not consist of doing only those things which God has not forbidden. It is not a matter of our clothes or the way we walk or in abstaining from food and drink. (All these things can be good if they are received gratefully and used reverently as blessings given to us by God.) Nobody who knows the truth will try to identify a Methodists by any of these outward appearances.

Nor are Methodists identified because they base their religion on any particular *part* of God's truth. By "salvation" the Methodist means holiness of heart and life. This springs from true faith and nothing else. Can even a nominal Christian deny this?

This concept of faith does not mean we are declaring God's Law to be void through faith. God forbid such a perverted conclusion! Instead we Methodists believe that faith is the means by which God's Law is established.

There are too many people who make a religion out of 1)

doing no harm or 2) doing good. (And often these two together.) God knows, we Methodists do not fall into this mistaken way of defining our Christianity! Experience proves that many people struggle vainly for a long, long time with this false idea of religion consisting of good works (or no bad works)! In the end these deluded people have no religion at all; they are not better off than when they started!

**THEN WHAT** *IS* THE DISTINGUISHING MARK OF A METHODIST? WHO *ARE* METHODISTS?

Methodists are people who have the love of God in their hearts. This is a gift of God's Holy Spirit. And the same Spirit causes Methodists to love the Lord their God with all their hearts, with all their souls, with all their minds, with all their strength.

God is the joy of Methodists' hearts; the desire of their souls, which cry out constantly, "Whom have I in heaven but you, Lord? There is nothing on earth that I desire but you, my God and my all! You are the strength of my life. You, Lord, are all that I need."

Naturally Methodists are happy in God. Yes, they are always happy because Methodists have within them that "well of water" which Christ promised. It floods up to overflowing, bringing glorious assurance of the life that never ends. Therefore, Methodists are persons in whom God's peace and joy are constantly evident.

Methodists do not fear God's wrath for themselves. Perfect love has banished fear of God's punishment from Methodists' hearts. For this reason they are able to rejoice evermore. They do not rejoice in themselves or in their achievements. Instead, Methodists rejoice in God who is their Lord and Savior.

Methodists acknowledge God as their Father. Why? Because Methodists have received from Jesus Christ the power to become glad and grateful children of the Father.

Methodists realize that they belong to God instead of Satan. This is redemption. It is possible only because Jesus

117

gave his life on the cross. He shed his blood to make atonement for the sins of all who believe in him. Methodists trust in Christ alone for their salvation. Methodists know that the blood of Jesus has cleansed them from all sin. Through Christ and Christ alone Methodists have received forgiveness for their sins.

Methodists never forget this. Methodists shudder as they consider the eternal punishment from which they have been delivered by Jesus Christ. Methodists give thanks that God loved them enough to spare them—to blot out their transgressions and iniquities . . . to atone for them with the shed blood and broken body of his beloved Son.

Having personally experienced deliverance from God's wrath, Methodists cannot help rejoicing. They rejoice every time they think of their narrow escape from eternal destruction. They rejoice that by God's kindness they, sinners, have been placed in a new and right relationship with their creator. This miracle has been accomplished through Jesus Christ, the beloved Savior.

Whoever thus believes experiences the assurance of God's love and forgiveness. This clear and certain inner recognition is witness that Methodists are children of God by faith. This truth is made known to Methodists as God sends his own Spirit to bear witness deep within the mind and soul of Methodists, enabling them to cry out "Father, my Father!" This is the inner witness of God's Holy Spirit, testifying to Methodists of their adoption into God's own family.

Methodists rejoice because they look forward confidently to seeing the glory of Christ fully revealed one day. This expectation is a source of great joy, and they exalt, "Blessed be the God and Father of our Lord Jesus Christ! According to the Father's abundant mercy he has caused me to be re-born so I can enjoy this eternal hope which never fades or tarnishes. This is an inheritance of faith. It cannot be stolen, lost or destroyed in any way. It is a pure and permanent hope. God has reserved its fulfillment in eternity for me!"

Having this great hope, Methodists give thanks to God at all times and in all circumstances. For Methodists know that God expects his children to be always grateful.

Methodists receive every happening cheerfully, declaring "Good is the will of the Lord." Whether the Lord gives or takes away, the Methodist blesses the name of the Lord.

Another characteristic of Methodists: They have learned to be content, whether they have much or little. When humiliation comes Methodists accept this gladly as the Father's will. When prosperity and good fortune come Methodists likewise give God the credit. Methodists accept all circumstances gladly, knowing that these are God's doing, intended for their ultimate good.

Whether they are in leisure or suffering pain . . . whether they are sick or in good health . . . whether they live or die, Methodists give thanks to God from the very depths of their hearts. For the Methodist trusts that God's ways are always good . . . that every wonderful and perfect gift comes to us from God, into whose providential hand the Methodist has committed his body and soul.

Methodists know no paralyzing frustration and anxiety! Methodists have thankfully cast their every care upon God, never failing to let God know all about their needs and problems.

Methodists never stop praying. It is second nature for them to pray and not to be discouraged. This does *not* mean that Methodists are always praying in a church building! (Though it goes without saying that the Methodist misses no opportunity for public worship.) Methodists are often on their knees in humility before God, but they do not spend all their time in contemplation.

Nor do Methodists try to beat God's ears with many words. For the Holy Spirit speaks to God on behalf of Methodists, expressing their innermost hopes and longings which human words cannot articulate. This alone is true prayer; the language of the heart which overflows with joy is sometimes best expressed in holy silence before God.

The Methodist's whole self is tuned to God's will—at all times, and in all circumstances. Nothing can sever the bond that unites the Methodist and God. This constant sense of closeness and communion cannot be broken by business, leisure or conversation. This closeness to God is the true sign of the Methodist's love for his or her Creator and Redeemer. Therefore, the Methodist walks with God, being constantly aware of him who is invisible and immortal.

Inscribed indelibly on the Methodist's heart is the truth that "he who loves God loves his brother also." This means that Methodists care about their neighbors as much as they care about themselves!

Their hearts are full of love—for everyone. This love does not stop with Methodists' personal acquaintances; it encircles all humanity. Even those who hate Methodists receive love in return. For like Jesus, the Methodist loves his or her enemies. And the Methodist loves even God's enemies, the evil and the unthankful. If Methodists cannot possibly do good to their enemies, still Methodists pray for those who trouble and insult them. This is what it means to be "pure in heart."

The Methodist can experience this purity because God has cleansed the Methodist's heart, washing away all urge for revenge . . . all envy . . . all wrath . . . all desire for harming another person. Every unkind inclination is gone . . . every evil lust and desire too. Pride has been purged out of the Methodist mind and heart. Gone also is haughtiness which always causes friction between people.

In place of these "human" weaknesses, the Methodist has taken the character of Christ. This is evident in a true Methodist's meekness . . . patience in the face of frustration . . . absence of pride . . . honest estimate of his or her own strengths and weaknesses.

If anybody causes them trouble, embarrassment or discomfort, Methodists can forgive. Because God, for the sake of Christ, has forgiven Methodists for their sins. All of this means that a Methodist never has reason to quarrel and fight with anybody, regardless how great the provocation. And why should Methodists fight? Nobody can take from them the things they consider most important: God and the things of God. Methodists are immune to conflict because they have crucified their "old selves" which used to be directed by the desires and the standards of the lower nature.

There is one great desire which motivates Methodists: to do not his or her own will but God's. The Methodist's single intention is to please God. This absorption with God fills the Methodist's life with radiance, joy and peace at all times. Because the Methodist is focused on God to the exclusion of all else, the light which is God fills the Methodist's whole being. Thus he or she is a child of Light.

So God reigns alone and supreme within the Methodist. No motion of the Methodist's mind or conscience is out of tune with God's gracious, sovereign will. A Methodist's every thought and action points to the Lord.

Anybody can identify a tree by its fruits. So also the Methodist is known because his or her life bears the fruit for God: keeping all the commandments from the greatest to the very least. The Methodist conscience is clear before God. Whatever God forbids, that the Methodist avoids. Whatever God has commanded, the Methodist does, whether this involves joy or grief, ease or great difficulty, gain or loss. Because the Methodist has been set at liberty by God's Spirit, he or she finds deepest satisfaction in doing God's will, on earth even as it is in heaven.

Methodists keep *all* God's commandments—not half-heartedly but with enthusiasm and gladness. The Methodists' obedience to God is in direct proportion to their love for God. And this "perfect love" is the source of Methodists' desire to obey God's Law one hundred percent.

All this means that Methodists are continually offering their whole selves to God . . . holding back nothing but giving all to increase the glory of God in the world.

Methodists know that every single ability comes from God. So Methodists gladly dedicate these talents to the Lord. Methodists withhold nothing from God . . . nothing. Before they became Christians, Methodists allowed evil to take control of their bodies and minds. Now, having died to the authority of sin, and having risen with Christ to a new and holy life, Methodists have given themselves over to God's control.

Not only do Methodists *aim* at complete dedication to God, they achieve this! Their businesses, their recreation, their social life all serve this great purpose: "Whatever you do, in word or in deed, do it all in the name of the Lord Jesus, giving thanks to God the Father through him."

The customs of this world don't prevent the Methodist from full dedication to God. He or she runs the race of daily life, knowing that God has ordained this as his or her calling. The Methodist knows that wickedness is wrong in the sight of God, even though society may consider it perfectly acceptable. The Methodist never forgets that someday everybody will have to account to God for every thought and every action.

Therefore, Methodists cannot follow the crowd when the crowd chooses to do evil. They cannot devote themselves to selfish indulgence. Methodists can no more be preoccupied with making money than they could swallow red hot embers! Nor can the Methodist waste money on fancy clothes or jewelry, which flatter the senses but do not glorify God at all.

Another mark of Methodists: They will not take part in any amusement which has the least possibility of causing harm to others. They cannot speak evil of his their neighbors any more than they can lie for God or any person. Love keeps guard over the Methodists' lips, so they cannot speak evil of anybody. Nor is God's precious gift of speech wasted with useless, inane chatter which does not help people in some constructive way.

Whatever things are pure and noble, on these the

Methodist fixes attention. Also on things that are lovely, just and of good reputation. Thus, all that the Methodist says or does somehow furthers the gospel of Jesus Christ.

As time permits, Methodists do good to all, their neighbors and strangers, their friends and enemies. This includes every kind of good. Naturally Methodists provide food for the hungry, clothing to the naked. They visits people who are sick and in prison. But even more important than this, Methodists labor to do good to the souls of people. According to the ability which God has given to them, Methodists labor to awaken those who have never known God and therefore sleep the slumber of eternal death. And when people are awakened to God, Methodists help them realize that the atoning blood of Jesus has power to cleanse away their sins. *The greatest good work a Methodist can do is to help somebody get into right relationship with God. For this is the only way a person can have peace with God.*

When Methodists meet somebody who has not yet found peace with God, Methodists stir them up in the hope that they may be set free to do the good works which God intends for every person to do.

Methodists are willing to spend their time and energies in doing this important work for God. Their time and talents are given as a loving sacrifice to God that the people round about them may grow into the fullness of Christ.

These are the principles and practices of Methodism. These are the marks of a true Methodist. By these things alone does the Methodist wish to be distinguished from others.

Somebody may say, "Why these are only the common, basic principles of Christianity!" This is what Methodism is, nothing more or less. We Methodists refuse to be distinguished from other men, by any other than the common principles of Christianity—the plain, old Christianity that I teach, renouncing and detesting all other marks of distinction. Any person who fits this pattern is a Christian no matter what you call him or her! It is not a matter of denominational label but of being inwardly and outwardly conformed to the will of God, as this is revealed in the Bible.

The Christian thinks, speaks and lives according to the pattern set by Jesus. And his or her soul is renewed in righteousness and holiness after God's own image.

By these marks we Methodists labor to distinguish ourselves from the unbelieving world, from all whose minds and lives are not ruled according to the gospel of Christ. But we Methodists do not wish to be distinguished at all from real Christians of any denomination. Like them we are seeking that perfection of Christ which we have not yet attained. As Jesus said—whoever does the will of the Heavenly Father is our brother, sister and mother.

And so I beg you, let all true Christians remain united; let us not be divided among ourselves. *Is your heart right as my heart is with yours? I ask no further question; give me your hand. For the sake of mere opinions or terms, let us not destroy the work of God.*

Do you love God? This is enough. I give you the right hand of fellowship.

"If there is any consolation in Christ . . . any comfort in love . . . any fellowship in the Spirit . . . any affection and sympathy," then let us work together in behalf of the gospel. Let us walk in a way that is worthy of the vocation in which we are called. Let us walk in lowliness and meekness with long-suffering, kindly sparing one another in love, trying always to keep the unity of the Spirit in the bond of peace. For we remember always that "there is one body and one Spirit . . . one hope to our calling; one Lord, one faith, one baptism, one God and Father of us all. He is above all things, through all things and in you as well."